# Youth policy in Albania

## Conclusions of the Council of Europe international review team

Howard Williamson (Rapporteur)

Zdeňka Mašková (Chair)
Imse Nilsson
Guy-Michel Brandtner
Filip Coussée
Srđ Kišević

Council of Europe Publishing

Cover photo: © Zdenka Maskova 2009
Cover design and layout: Documents and Publications Production Department (SPDP), Council of Europe


Council of Europe Publishing
F-67075 Strasbourg Cedex
http://book.coe.int

ISBN 978-92-871-6823-8
© Council of Europe, July 2010
Printed at the Council of Europe

# Contents

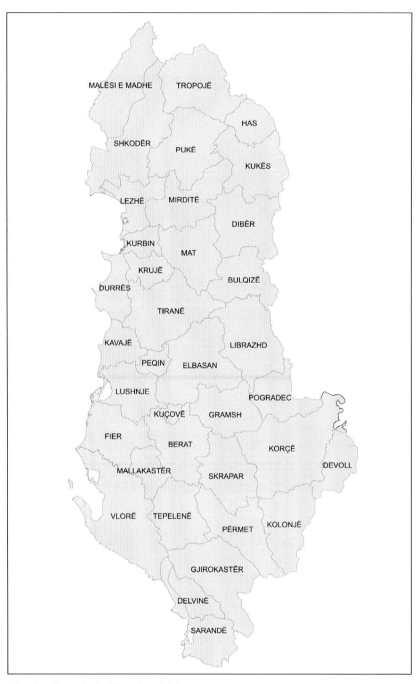

*Albania – Map of administrative divisions*

# Summary

This is the seventeenth in a series of international reviews of national youth policy conducted by the Council of Europe since 1997. The international review team visited Albania twice in 2009 and a national hearing on its conclusions was held in Tirana in February 2010.

The framework of the review was a little different from preceding reviews and can be considered as a "third stage" in an evolving review process. The first stage was somewhat ad hoc until, after seven reviews, a synthesis of the findings to that point was produced, and a framework to guide future reviews was suggested. This framework was broadly followed for the next seven reviews, when a further synthesis added significantly to the framework of issues that any review should be attentive to. However, this created an almost unmanageable task, unless the reviews spread their attention very thinly and failed to offer any real depth to their analyses. Hence the changed approach for the international review of youth policy in Albania. Though it continued to explore briefly the range of policy domains and cross-cutting issues that had been identified for the earlier framework, these were used more to set the scene and context rather than to present an analysis. The analysis was focused much more on three issues identified a priori by the Albanian authorities (suggested during a preliminary visit that took place in January 2009 and following a practice that was first established during the 8th review of Lithuania in 2002) and three issues that were viewed as important priorities by the international review team. This was the significant departure from previous review processes and may be the approach adopted in the future.

A further departure that was not, however, a precedent for future international youth policy reviews was the acceptance that Albania need not produce its own national youth policy report ahead of the visit by the international review team. This had, until this point, always been the practice of all previous international reviews (though some countries produced only draft reports and did not complete their national reports until after the international reports had been submitted, leading to some concerns about inappropriate political tactics). In 2006, Albania had produced a National Youth Strategy for 2007-13 and, given the pressures on the Youth Department within the Ministry of Tourism, Culture, Youth and Sports during an election year in 2009, it was felt that the strategy was a sufficient baseline to "anchor" the deliberations of the international review.

The international review itself took place during two week-long visits in September and November 2009. It met with officials from various ministries, the Youth Minister himself, numerous youth NGOs, many projects aimed at young people and young people themselves. The first visit was concentrated on policy and provision within the central administration and in the capital city. The second visit sought to understand the experience of youth practitioners and young people beyond Tirana, in places such as Durrës, Fier, Shkodra and Bushat.

The international report starts with a preface of general observations both about the international youth policy review process and the specific experiences of the international review team in Albania. The first substantive chapter is concerned with providing some contextual information about Albania, the country, and about the National Youth Strategy. Chapter 2 seeks to present some brief understanding of the broad range of issues affecting young people in Albania, across specific policy domains (such as education and health), in relation to particular groups (such as minorities and those with disabilities), in the context of key cross-cutting issues (such as mobility or social inclusion), and on particular issues (such as the environment). This is no more than a cursory journey designed to inform the reader of the general "condition" of young people and youth policy in Albania today.

The key substantive chapters follow. Chapter 3 covers the three key issues that were suggested by the Albanian government as matters of particular concern: the legislative framework, delivery mechanisms and youth participation. Concerns are expressed about the proliferation of legislation yet apparently limited implementation. This was a recurrent criticism and merits serious attention. Delivery mechanisms have yet to be properly established and there is still too much reliance on the ad hoc initiatives of youth NGOs, committed individuals and the interest in youth issues amongst some municipalities. However, developments in youth participation are considered to be the jewel in the crown of Albanian youth policy: only a few years ago, an impressive range of "stepping stones" (children's governments in schools, youth parliaments in local communities, and student councils) for the expression of young voices and platforms for youth activity were developed almost from scratch.

Chapter 4 discusses the three issues that emerged during the international youth policy review process as being of particular interest to the international review team: youth information, leisure time and youth justice. There is concern that numerous calls for improved information provision, both for youth practitioners and for young people, are insufficiently grounded in clear thinking about the role and purpose of such provision. So, although there is certainly a need for more structured channels of communication and information, sharper preliminary thinking is definitely required. The international review team was also concerned at the absence of what might be called "associational" space for young people. Spaces for young people to gather, converse and have fun, without necessarily having to be part of formal structures or involved in preparing for and executing projects, are important for youth development and for working out (and, where there is tension with other members of local communities, working through) young people's social relationships – between themselves and with others – within their localities. In terms of youth justice, rather like the progress on youth participation outlined above, there have been dramatic developments in recent years, with the establishment of a dedicated youth correctional facility and the emergence of more community-based sentencing of young offenders.

The report concludes with a reflective discussion of the strengths and weaknesses of contemporary youth policy in Albania. The direction of travel is commendable and the National Youth Strategy says all the right things but, though it is a useful blueprint, the pace of development on different issues has been highly variable, with virtually nothing happening on some fronts and striking progress on others. There is a tentative glance towards the future because it is reassuring that many young Albanians are now reasonably positive about their future and the future of their country – though they would like more investment in their futures. Finally, there is an assertion that – within a country that only a few years ago could hardly have been thinking of "youth policy" at all during a climate of political and economic chaos and where many young people simply wanted to leave – "hope dies last": the Albanian Youth Council has just been re-established after a hiatus of some four years and there is an inherent optimism that things will steadily get better for a population of young people in one of the youngest countries in Europe.

The recommendations of the review are gathered together at the end of the report.

That over 300 people, of whom well over half were young people, attended the national hearing to debate and comment on the findings of the international review for three hours and more reflects a deep national interest in the prospects for young people in Albania and suggests that there is the energy, understanding and commitment to take things further forward. The media also appears to be interested in youth policy issues and developments. The international review team hopes that stronger collaboration and communication between political structures, the public administration, youth NGOs and young people themselves will bring more concrete action into effect. There is no shortage of ideas and aspirations; the test now is to establish more robust structures and the capacity and competence to turn impressive rhetoric into actuality.

# Preface

> There seemed no escape from the country's escalating spiral of woes ... The young
> wanted to get out at any cost and did not mind where. (Vickers 2008, p. 233)

It is little more than 10 years since Albania faced economic and political meltdown
following the pyramid selling scandal and a sequence of unstable governments.
It is less than 20 years since Albania emerged from 50 years of isolation as a
non-revisionist communist system led for most of that time by its brutal yet
charismatic leader Enver Hoxha, "whose complex and contradictory personality
had forged a unique and lonely path for Albania, and left its imprint on every
aspect of Albanian life" (Vickers 2008, p. 209). Albania was the last of the
European socialist countries to break with communism (De Waal 2007). Hoxha
himself died only a quarter of a century ago – one generation. A decade ago, the
solution, if that is the word, to the country's multiple problems seemed to lie in
mass emigration, an entrenched poverty for most of those who remained, apart
from the relative affluence of a small elite supported by nepotistic networks and
fuelled by corruption. Some of this has not changed, but the progressive
changes since that time are palpable, bringing a recent British newspaper article
to conclude that Albania could, indeed perhaps should, be on the verge of
becoming the 28th member of the European Union:

> Albania? ... There's an energy and a sense of progress here that catches you by the
> throat. A small, impoverished country with an improbable Stalinist history is turning
> its 17 years of freedom into something remarkable ...
>
> Talk to witnesses from round the Balkans and the EU is the first answer on their lips.
> Make us more secure. Give us a settled fabric for trade and aid. Help us to feel something
> more than an agglomeration of spare parts stuck on the end of a continent. And let
> us feel that if we make the progress you require, it will be rewarded ...
>
> A union of 34 countries or more? It's coming, through a veil of sneers. And if you still
> need a battered vision to cherish, come to Tirana's Skanderbeg Square and find a
> little hope amongst the potholes. (*Guardian*, 23 November 2009)

European Union accession may still be some way off, but Albania's status as a
newly acknowledged candidate country is indeed recognition of its modernisation

in recent years and growing adherence to the rule of law (though we might suggest almost too many laws), human rights (though there remain many questions) and an emergent and recognisable democracy (though it is fragile). These are the central tenets of the work of the Council of Europe, of which Albania has been a member since 1995, and which has been conducting reviews of national youth policies by international review teams since 1997. Albania is the 17th country to volunteer for such a reviewing process.[1]

Following a meeting of participants in some of the recent reviews in The Hague in December 2008, to consider the future development of the review process, it was decided that the youth policy review of Albania should forge a "third" step in the approach. Initially, during the reviews that took place between 1997 and 2001, each review essentially followed its own path, preferences and priorities. A comparative synthesis of these first seven reviews (Williamson 2002) pointed to this diversity but suggested, from the grounded evidence available from the seven national reports as well as the seven international reports, that there was a framework that might be followed to guide the practice of future reviews. In short, this captured some six key "ingredients" of youth policy: concepts (of "youth" and "youth policy"), enabling structures (legislation and budget), delivery mechanisms (including the work of youth organisations), domains of youth policy (such as education and health), cross-cutting issues (such as social inclusion or mobility), and supporting structures (such as youth research and professional training). Following a second synthesis of the next seven international reviews (Williamson 2008), the detail of this framework was further elaborated, to include a range of themes and issues that had not been evident in the earlier reviews: such as the role of the church and military service in "youth policy", and the negative mobility arising from the trafficking in women and the movement of illegal migrant labour (that usually included significant numbers of young people). However, to expect the next "wave" of international reviews to cover this agenda comprehensively was considered by The Hague meeting to be quite unrealistic; it would spread the focus too thinly. The important point was that the whole of this package was relevant to consideration of youth policy. For Albania, it was felt that the "test-bedding" of a new approach to priorities would be adopted, taking the priorities of the government as a starting point (which had been the practice since 2002 – see below) but permitting the international review team to identify its handful of key themes as well. This approach was duly followed.

Another point of departure from the custom and practice of the review process since its start was the acceptance of no preceding national report. It must be emphasised, however, that this was not a new precedent but simply a pragmatic concession to the very limited human resources of the Youth Department in

1. The other countries to have been subject to Council of Europe international reviews of national youth policy are: Finland, the Netherlands, Sweden, Spain, Romania, Estonia, Luxembourg, Lithuania, Norway, Malta, Slovakia, Cyprus, Armenia, Latvia, Hungary, and Moldova.

Albania, coupled with the fact that the review took place around a national election, when clearly other demands were placed upon the staff of the ministry. Moreover, a comprehensive National Youth Strategy for 2007-13 had been published at the end of 2006 (Ministry of Tourism, Culture, Youth and Sports 2006) and this was considered to be an adequate substitute – as an anchor point of information on Albanian youth policy for the international review team – for a national youth policy report.

Otherwise, the Albania review followed a now established path: a preliminary visit took place in January 2009, confirming governmental youth policy priorities to which the ministry wanted the international review team to give attention and outlining mutual expectations and responsibilities; a week-long first visit in September 2009, consisting mainly of securing an understanding of "top-down" perspectives from the government and national (and international) NGOs; a second visit in November 2009, also for a week, seeking to grasp more "bottom-up" perspectives through visits to projects and organisations both in Tirana and beyond; and scheduled national and international hearings in February and March 2010 respectively, following the production of a draft and then a final international report. It was in between the two visits by the international review team that the team identified its own three priority issues (youth information, leisure time and youth justice) to supplement and complement those already indicated by the Albanian government (legislation, delivery structures and youth participation). Following some general contextual discussion, both of Albania in general and the situation of its young people in particular, this report will focus on these in turn, starting with the government's agenda and followed by those of particular interest to the international review team.

One of the unplanned but always hoped-for consequences of these youth policy reviews is the recognition and value conveyed by a team of international visitors, from six different countries, endorsed by the Council of Europe, to the hard work and often phenomenal commitment of enthusiastic people, usually volunteers, seeking to effect change and improve the lives of young people and their communities at the very local level. Such individuals and organisations are often working in quite adverse conditions, yet displaying great resourcefulness and resilience despite such circumstances. The international review team was especially conscious of this in Albania.

A more personal effect of being part of an international policy review team is that you become forever fascinated by the country in question; you can never again watch TV, surf the Net, or read a newspaper without being drawn to any coverage, on any matter at all, that relates to that country. The country, in some ways, becomes a surrogate home. So it was perhaps appropriate that the international review team was accommodated, on its second visit, in Hotel California, almost next to the ministry, evoking the lines from The Eagles' song of the same name: "you can check out any time you want, but you can never leave"! Albania will be "with" each member of the international review team for the rest of our lives.

Preface

11

For some members of any international review team, it is their first visit to the country in focus. This produces a very demanding learning curve, particularly around gaining an understanding of culture, politics and history, and this was an especially acute challenge in the context of Albania. It was therefore extremely valuable for the team to have visited the youth NGO project MOKO (Museum of the Objects of Communism) to gain some sense of Albania's relatively recent history. The notes of that visit capture our impressions but also convey something of the "education" we received that afternoon.

## Visit to youth project MOKO (Museum of the Objects of Communism)

There is a fascinating commitment and aspirations to develop both exhibition and education on the "ordinary" lives of people under the old regime. Many artefacts are being collected. Kerosene cans for cooking in the bathroom. Radios that played illegal music quietly, positioned in the middle of the room so neighbours could not hear. There were few children's toys, except dolls. There was a mythology of progress through "new inventions", when in fact items were imported from abroad (Russia and then later China). People collected Coke cans at the tourist seaside, to use as salt dispensers and ornaments. The Best of Deep Purple on what would have been an illegal Sony HF60 cassette tape. Old bicycle pumps.

There is hope of saving some of slogans that have been layered on the walls throughout Tirana. The intention is to transform two flats into a museum of everyday life, educating children and perhaps attracting older people who lived through those times and triggering their memories, possibly producing the opportunity to record those memories as oral history.

The project is still very much in the development stage, but three very committed individuals are giving their time and resources to the project and hope it will start operating on a reasonably solid basis sometime in the spring of 2010. There does not appear to be a lot of interest or support from the Culture Ministry or the Municipality of Tirana, but it is certainly a very fascinating initiative from the perspective of the international review team.

The team was composed, as usual, of six people. Two were the nominees of the statutory bodies of the Youth Directorate of the Council of Europe (the CDEJ, the European Steering Committee for Youth Co-operation in Europe, representing governments; and the Advisory Council for Youth, representing youth organisations) and another represented the Secretariat. The remaining three members of a team are usually youth researchers but, on this occasion, it proved impossible to find such an individual from the Balkan region ("local" knowledge is deemed to be important) and so eventually a member of a political youth organisation who came from Croatia supplemented the other two youth researchers, one of whom co-ordinated the review and served as rapporteur.

The international review team would like to express and extend its thanks to all those it met during its two visits to Albania. During the preliminary visit – made by the co-ordinator and the Secretariat – we were impressed by the endeavours to "make youth policy together" and indeed we coined the concept of "ensemble", given that the Deputy Minister at the time was also the conductor of an orchestra. There are, of course, huge challenges to doing this in every country, but even its expression in Albania – as we note further in our conclusion – is an extremely positive sign both of progress and commitment.

We had a good programme (see Appendix 1 and Appendix 2) that served the team well, kept to time and addressed the range of topics in which we were interested. There were some "blips" to the timetable and visits to projects where we had anticipated something different (such as the "community project" that turned out to be a "special school" – a provision for children and young people with special needs – on the last Friday of the second visit), but by and large we maximised our learning opportunities on matters of interest to ourselves and the government. As there is a public holiday at the end of November, there were some difficulties having contact with some groups we would have liked to have talked to (such as another community project to which we had been invited during the first visit and youth researchers – if they really exist in Albania). We also recognise that an international review can provide valuable public relations opportunities for politicians at all levels and, at times, we were not immune to that motive. It was also sometimes rather difficult to discern what was in the past, what currently prevailed and what was in visions and plans. Clearly there are still some powerful legacies of the past – traditions do die hard – that have not yet been completely eradicated or revised (and some, arguably, should not be), there are claims about contemporary provision that rarely seem to stretch beyond either the capital city or at least some of the larger towns and there are numerous commendable aspirations that are yet to see any concrete reality. But, like all international youth policy reviews, we have had to work with what we were told, in the context of wider reading done by members of the team and have had to make our judgments and draw our conclusions accordingly. We have to admit to some disappointment that invitations to follow up by e-mail with more detailed issues raised in face-to-face discussions were not taken up, even when individuals and organisations signalled their intention to write and indeed promised to do so; in our view, this was an opportunity missed for two reasons: first, the international review team has no intention of airing unsubstantiated assertions and allegations on behalf of any group and second, there was a commitment to incorporate any written submissions into the body of this report. If individuals and groups are so vocal and often one-dimensional in their verbal concerns, then some written support is essential to validate their case.

We were fortunate to be in Albania's capital for the opening day of the Tirana International Film Festival. The Youth Department kindly invited the team to attend the showing of *Honeymoons*, the first film to be supported co-operatively by the Serbian and Albanian governments which, in recent years, were at odds

– almost as ever historically – over Kosovo,[2] a central sub-theme to the film. For the international review team, however, the film was symbolic in a different way. Though we watched it in the National Theatre, it was still a film and its focus was significantly about the question of access to the European Union. During the international review, the two recurrent themes raised by young people were the "visa problem" and the lack of access to cinemas – and so the film carried, for us, a particular and very contemporary relevance.

Though we have already thanked all of our respondents collectively, the international review team wishes to express its gratitude to both the Youth Department (more correctly, the Directory of Co-ordination of Youth Policies) within the Ministry of Tourism, Culture, Youth and Sports, and the Council of Europe Information Office in Tirana. Both interpersonally and logistically, the hospitality extended by their staff and their commitment to the organisation of our visits made the review process both professional and rewarding.

Following the national hearing, which was held at the beginning of February 2010 with well over 300 participants (including a significant proportion of young people) in attendance, the Minister for Tourism, Culture, Youth and Sports re-affirmed to the international review team his deep commitment – as a parliamentarian and citizen, as well as a minister – to Albania's youth policy agenda. He welcomed the critical observations (as well as the positive commendations!) made verbally during the presentation of the review to the national hearing. In order to strengthen the instruments to "move things forward", he informed the international review team that he had elevated the former Youth Director to the position of Director-General for Youth and Sports (thus embedding the profile of "youth" more deeply within the ministry), appointed a Director for Youth Policy, and added two more specialists to the youth team within the ministry. He hoped this would speed up the establishment of a National Centre for Youth (referred to in this review as the National Youth Centre), bring about some significant "quick wins" in the implementation of youth policy, and improve co-ordination across ministries and between the government and the regions – in his view, the most central challenge for improving both the structures and the delivery of youth policy in Albania.

---

2. All references to Kosovo, whether to the territory, institutions or population, in this text, shall be understood in full compliance with United Nations Security Council Resolution 1244 and without prejudice to the status of Kosovo.

# 1. introduction — Albania and the National Youth Strategy

## "A country full of surprises and of the unexpected"

One member of the international review team, also from a country with a state socialist past, expressed admiration of Albania for the way it had slowly been able to rid itself of "the communist heritage inflicted on the souls of the people". There has been a continuing evolution of the legislative and civil society environment which, though far from ideal, is a far cry from the system that prevailed less than 20 years ago. During the period of the international review Albania became a candidate country for the European Union, the National Youth Council was in the process of being resurrected, and a National Youth Agency/ Centre was being planned by the ministry. This reflects the character of a country constantly trying to deal with relationships between traditions and change. Two cameos highlighted this point: the frequent references to changing the mentality of Albanian youth (towards a more independent and "entrepreneurial" future), and the farmer in Bushat who talked about the contemporary importance of economic collectives in rural areas, a difficult concept given the specificities of Albania's relatively recent past. There is a need both to move forward and to reclaim elements of the past. One problem is the kinds of role models that now prevail in Albanian society. We heard from an international NGO that, before the 1990s, teachers used to be thought of as "second mothers" who were highly respected: "after the changes, they became poor public employees and are despised". There was now no possibility in Albania for moral authority to be divorced from economic power; the two allegedly went hand in hand! Celebrity culture had been imported from neighbouring countries. One respondent said that capitalism should be defined in terms of respect for the law and making money, but "the former is often lost" (see Chapter 3). A student with an Audi A4 has no respect for a professor with an old car: "the professor no longer has any moral authority". An activist within a youth NGO observed that young people's aspirations "are usually just related to jobs that pay very good money". The moral compass in Albania is therefore still very narrowly conceived. Even in relation to the overarching goals of European integration – and in the context of

Albania's very youthful society – the Ministry of Integration was rather dismissive of a youth agenda: "Youth is not a priority in the *acquis communautaire*". And so it was unimportant! The narrow mind-set sometimes attributed to young people is certainly not exclusive to them.

In the late 20th century there was a palpable failure amongst many foreigners to "distinguish between Albania's economic level – on a par with that of some third world countries – and the educational and cultural (music, art, literature, theatre) standard which was as good or better than that of a number of the first world countries" (De Waal 2007, p. 2). This is the paradox of Albania and one which, as a result, produces a country full of surprises.

The Republic of Albania is a parliamentary democracy established under a constitution that was renewed in 1998. Its geographical neighbours are Italy (a short distance across the sea), Montenegro, Kosovo, the Former Yugoslav Republic of Macedonia, and Greece. It has a population of some 3.6 million people. Of these, some 600 000 live in the capital Tirana (though some sources put this figure at 800 000 and others at 350 000!). Albania became an independent country in 1912, following 500 years of Ottoman domination. For over 40 years Albania's territorial integrity was preserved by the communist regime, though at a terrible cost to the population, which was subjected to purges, shortages, repression of civil and political rights, a total ban on religious observance, and increasing isolation. The Euro-Atlantic integration of Albania – to improve economic conditions and bring about basic democratic reforms, including a multi-party system – has been the ultimate goal of the post-communist governments. As the economy develops migration has slowed, though the country remains relatively poor by European standards (per capita income was about US$3 500 in 2008, an average salary around €300 a month, and almost 20% of the population live below the poverty line, according to the World Bank, while unemployment, almost certainly underestimated, is usually put at around 15%). As a result, many Albanians continue to migrate to Greece, Italy, Germany, other parts of Europe and to North America. Economic progress is hampered by a large informal economy (estimated by some to be as large as 50% of official GDP) and an inadequate energy and transportation infrastructure. The economy is, however, bolstered by annual remittances from abroad, estimated to be in the region of US$600-800 million. Agriculture, which accounts for more than one fifth of GDP, is held back because of a lack of modern equipment, unclear property rights and the prevalence of small, inefficient plots of land. Energy shortages and antiquated and inadequate infrastructure contribute to Albania's poor business environment, which makes it difficult to attract and sustain foreign investment.

Following the end of communism, the democratically elected government, which won the elections in 1992, embarked on a radical and ambitious economic reform programme. This included a comprehensive package of structural reforms including privatisation, enterprise, financial sector reform and the creation of the legal framework for a market economy and private sector activity. Successive governments have had to try to deal with high unemployment, widespread corruption, a dilapidated physical infrastructure, powerful organised crime networks and usually combative political opponents. The Stabilisation and Association Agreement of 2006 supported the pursuance of wider reforms, including the freedom of the press, property rights, institution building, respecting ethnic minorities and observing international standards in municipal elections. There have been recent improvements in the country's infrastructure and communications networks.

The average age of the Albanian population is around 32 years. Albania is a largely ethnically homogeneous country (some 95% are ethnic Albanians) with only small minorities, who include Greeks, Aromanians (Vlachs), Torbesh, Gorani, Macedonians, Roma, Montenegrins, Bulgarians, Balkan Egyptians and Jews.

An independent Albania has never had an official state religion; all regimes since 1912 have followed a systematic policy of separating religion from official functions and cultural life. During the communist period, the state policy was to obliterate all religion completely, through suppressing religious observance and institutions. Albania was declared to be the world's first atheist state. Religious freedom returned in 1992 and most Albanians are Muslim (approximately 70%), though there are some Orthodox Christians (approximately 20%) in the south-east of the country and Roman Catholics (approximately 10%) in the extreme north. Religious extremism and discrimination are very rare.

Albania is divided into 12 administrative divisions or regions/counties, officially known as qarkut, though these are often also known as prefektura. There are 36 districts and 351 municipalities. Each region has a regional council and is composed of a number of municipalities and "communes" (or komuna), which are the first level of local governance responsible for local needs and law enforcement.

Two of Albania's greatest achievements have been its provision of education and health services, where there is a literacy rate of around 90% (though this conceals significant gender differences) and a life expectancy approaching 80 years. Two of its major concerns are the trafficking in persons (for the purposes of prostitution, forced labour and begging), of whom about half the victims are under the age of 18, and Albania's place as a trans-shipment point for illegal drugs and the money laundering associated with these practices.[3]

## The National Youth Strategy

The long transition in Albania altered with deep political and socio-economic crisis in the last 15 years brought dramatic changes: immediate opening of the country, clashing values and beliefs, deterioration of educational and social services, increasing unemployment and poverty; all these put the Albanian society and Albanian youth in particular to new and complex challenges. (Albanian Association of Psychologists 2008)

---

3. Sources: Albania – Wikipedia (2009); The World Factbook (2009); U.S. Department of State (2008); Foreign and Commonwealth Office (2009); BBC (2009); Facts about Albania (2009).

Albania has one of the highest birth rates and is the second youngest country in Europe (after Kosovo) and its youth population is close to 70% of the total but, despite this proportion and the predictable rhetoric of many of those we spoke to, young people were often considered to be "not a priority" amongst the country's current challenges and issues. In some pivotal sectors of government, this position took us completely by surprise! But clearly, despite the truism, Albania's future lies in the hands of its young people, and its National Youth Strategy (Ministry of Tourism, Culture, Youth and Sports 2006, p. 7) proclaims

> the need to delineate a strategic platform for the sustainable development of youth that is consistent with the priorities of the new government and resonant with the socio-economic and cultural transformations that have taken place during the last few years. At the heart of this initiative lies the idea that younger generations in Albania represent key agents for positive change towards the consolidation of democratic governance and the process of European integration.

Specific aspects of the National Youth Strategy, those most pertinent to the issues under discussion, will be identified below. Suffice it to note here some of the overarching elements of the strategy. Its contents (with most sections divided into four: a situation analysis; vision, priorities and strategic goals; policies; and resources and indicators) cover the following areas:

–   inter-sectorial co-ordination and collective involvement;

–   representation and participation of young people;

–   youth and economy;

–   health and social protection;

–   recreation and free time;

–   Albanian youth: future European citizens;

–   priority programmes for National Youth Strategy;

–   National Youth Action Plan.

The key cross-cutting messages that thread through many of the areas outlined above and emerge from the strategy are as follows:

–   collaboration and co-operation (between ministries and NGOs);

–   participation, democracy and empowerment;

–   information and research;

–   exchange and internationalism;

–   the sustainability and strength of NGOs;

–   prevention, protection, promotion.

This is an impressive strategic framework for youth policy, but recurrent concerns were expressed about its realism and its prospects for serious follow-up and implementation. Indeed, some respondents were eager to inform the international review team that, although in the recent elections (in the summer of 2009) youth issues were reasonably prominent – particularly education and employment – there was hardly a mention of the National Youth Strategy. Like too many government strategies, there were serious doubts expressed by many respondents that the strategy would forge a path towards practical action and implementation.[4]

According to the Youth Department, responsibility for the implementation of programmes linked to the National Youth Strategy is distributed across different ministries, with an employment project being led by the Ministry of Labour and various school-based initiatives being co-ordinated by the Ministry of Education. It is, however, the Ministry of Tourism, Culture, Youth and Sports that carries the responsibility for revising and developing the biennial updating of the National Action Plan – the operational dimension of the strategy – and, to that end, it requires other collaborating ministries to provide reports on operational progress. There was at least strong rhetorical belief in the effectiveness of this cross-governmental collaboration ("if it is written in Albania, it will have to work", said one official with a surprising level of conviction), even if there was more reticence about the capacity of NGOs to contribute reliably to the active development and progress of the strategy, largely because of their funding uncertainties (see below).[5]

Despite the many challenges and obstacles that lie in the way of making the commendable aspirations of the National Youth Strategy some kind of reality for the majority of young people in Albania, the international review team was struck almost immediately by the liberal mind-set that seems to prevail, almost irrespective of some of the more entrenched political positions. This open-mindedness on social questions was confirmed by subsequent experience. Unlike other countries, Albania does not face the barriers that are so often erected by the church on

---

4. The ministry wished to record that immediately after the elaboration of the National Youth Strategy a donors' conference had been organised to explore how the strategy could be supported. Reference was made to stronger guidelines for providing financial support to youth NGOs. The ministry also drew attention to the "many studies" that have been undertaken to support the objectives and implementation of the National Youth Strategy. Examples provided were studies of health behaviour among school children, risk behaviour among 18-year-olds, and substance abuse. The international review team had not been notified of these studies during the review process.

5. The ministry wanted to stress that in order to strengthen support for youth NGOs, the Albanian government had established the Agency for Civil Society to enable NGOs to be more active and to have fewer funding uncertainties. At the time of writing (February 2010) the international review team was informed that the agency was in the process of recruiting staff and its board was already in place. With regard to cross-government co-operation, the ministry also wished to emphasise that significant progress had been made in the past year (2009), especially after new structures had been established. In order to meet the obligations foreseen within a range of strategies, inter-ministerial groups had been created and there had been an increase in human resources "for the well-functioning of cross-governmental co-operation".

matters such as sexual health education. There is a willingness to think flexibly and responsively to "old" issues such as the blood-feuds in the north and to "new" issues such as intravenous drug use. It may be no surprise that faith groups in Albania wield relatively limited influence since, under Hoxha, it was a coerced atheist state and 60% of the population remain self-declared atheists. But there is also an apparent lack of moral or religious opposition from parents or other institutions to issues such as addressing sexual reproductive health in schools, which elsewhere have been a matter of significant controversy.

This commendation of the scope for 'sensible thinking' is, of course, subject to numerous caveats. Resources remain very thin and the political wind shifts frequently, changing priorities and the allocation of resources that are available. Perhaps of greater importance for youth policy, the centre-periphery or urban-rural divide is massive. Tirana is Tirana, and elsewhere is elsewhere. It is a world-over truth that rural areas are always more conservative, but the division in Albania is striking. Even in the Durrës region, adjacent to Tirana, the Youth Parliament spoke of the difficulties of engaging with parents from outside the conurbation of Durrës itself. Rolling out youth policy beyond the capital city and winning the hearts and minds of those with more traditional perspectives will remain a huge challenge for the foreseeable future.

# 2. The social condition of young people in Albania and an overview of youth policy

> "... not a very happy life, nor an unhappy one ... it is a routine life. Our age is full of stress. We are an age of contradictions. We say something thinking why didn't I say something else." (village girl, aged 15, Kavaja)
>
> (Institute for Development of Research and Alternatives 2008, p. 44)

The Institute for Development of Research and Alternatives (2008) report suggests that there has been a significant increase in the happiness of children and young people in Albania over recent years. In six years during the past decade, the number of happy children has increased from under half to just over two thirds, and those who are happy are more likely to be in school! Friends, family, school and leisure time all contribute, in relatively equal measure, to the happiness of Albanian children. This is an important finding to report before embarking on some more critical perspectives on the lives of young people in Albania and the contribution of these key socialising influences on those lives.

This international review is designed to debate some "core issues" identified by the government and by the international review team itself. However, inevitably, the team gleaned a broader insight into the lives of young people, the framework of youth policy, and the interface between the two. This chapter endeavours to provide an overview of what the team learned, using the established framework for earlier Council of Europe youth policy reviews, but covering the policy domains more briefly.

Prior to embarking on discussions with ministries, NGOs and others across different policy arenas, the team asked the Youth Department to delineate some of the most pertinent issues affecting young people and youth policy in Albania. Unlike many other European countries, there was not an immediate launch into the challenges of drugs and crime; indeed, it was asserted that there was a relatively small problem of substance misuse and that though crime was frequently discussed on TV, it was usually concerned with extreme levels of criminality such as murder. Serious offending and more petty crime were relatively uncommon. More concern was expressed about young people having "nothing to do" (an issue later corroborated as a key theme for the international review team), especially those who had withdrawn from formal schooling, and there were current efforts to promote what was referred to as "informal education" across Albania and to further encourage the work of NGOs working in the field of vocational education. The availability of appropriate or "acceptable" jobs was considered to be a key youth issue: "young people can find jobs, but they cannot find a proper job". Young people often possessed high levels of qualification but were "too young" to challenge for levels of work that matched these credentials. Family life was another issue, linked to the lack of suitable housing for young people. It was too expensive to live independently and so young people continue to live with their parents, often even after getting married. Parents and families were usually accepting of this – it was part of tradition with a family-centred culture – but young people were less and less enamoured with being "trapped" in this way.

Beyond the specific issues outlined above, the international review team was told that it remained a "big challenge" to engage the commitment of youth NGOs and to ensure their sufficient financing. There was also the issue of becoming "more present" in-other cities and areas beyond Tirana, though the ministry was pleased to note that there is now a "presence" in 12 cities and that meetings had been organised with young people in youth councils and youth parliaments in other cities.[6] But there are still no local youth strategies, which clearly makes the question of the delivery of youth policy a huge one.[7] The ministry was indeed insistent that the National Youth Strategy sought to involve local authorities across the 12 prefectures (regions) of Albania and, to that end, was in the process of establishing 12 "youth centres" to take the strategy closer to its constituency throughout the country.

## Education

"Not going to school is a bad thing because school is the most important thing about a child." (village girl, aged 10, Tirana)

"In these times you cannot go anywhere without education. The high school is the minimum you can do and it is necessary even for a low-paid job." (high-school boy, aged 16, Shkodra)

---

6. The ministry wished to register that the Albanian Youth Council had been reactivated on 21 November 2009 and had re-established youth centres in the whole of Albania through partnership with local NGOs and local governance structures. Following this, the Albanian Youth Council and the ministry have already started some common projects.

7. The ministry noted that there are two pilot projects on youth employment in Kukes and Shkodra, financed by an employment fund modelled on the European Social Fund.

"Not only in our school, but in the whole education system in Albania, there is an 'elite' of students that is treated good, while the other students are not treated fairly." (high-school boy, aged 17, Selenica)

(Institute for Development of Research and Alternatives 2008, p. 64)

One area where the Communist regime did make significant progress was in the field of education. Before the war Albania was the only country in Europe without a university. From 1945 the campaign against illiteracy was relentlessly waged by enrolling thousands of people in night schools, where they progressed from elementary classes to secondary courses … the virtual eradication of illiteracy must be considered one of the most impressive achievements of the Hoxha years. By 1963 every man and woman in the country was obliged to complete eight years of elementary schooling. (Vickers 2008, p. 199)

The success of Hoxha's campaign to eliminate illiteracy and introduce universal education was an extraordinary achievement given the very high previous level of illiteracy and the extreme poverty of the country. (De Waal 2007, p. 80)

The international review team was struck by the universality of educational and achievement dreams of young people, irrespective of the "types" of young people we spoke to: young prisoners, young Roma people or members of youth parliaments. We found that 89% of Albanian children attend school; 8% of children work, as do 35% of children who do not attend school. Most children say they have a "very good" or "good" relationship with teachers and schoolmates (Institute for Development of Research and Alternatives 2008). There appears to be a phenomenal thirst for learning and qualifications, even if desperate parents sometimes dissuade their children from continuing their education in order to make a living (of some – any – kind). Otherwise, parents appear to support this educational commitment by their children. And this is despite growing awareness and concern about over-qualification at the level of higher education – there are too many graduates and not enough graduate level jobs.

Schooling is compulsory for nine years (an extra year was added recently), from the age of six to 15. The curriculum is currently undergoing some dramatic reform, with a required common core, further elective options and also a range of extra-curricular subjects (which are decided upon by students at the beginning of each school year). However, despite education being a legal requirement, some 20% of young people stop at the age of 14, about half to work and the other half because there are no suitable schools in their vicinity; in response to the latter issue, there is a commitment to dormitory (residential) provision, which the international review team witnessed during a visit to a "professional" (vocational) school.

There is an impressive array of educational development within both the years of compulsory schooling and beyond. Education for all has always been "part of the system", but now there is renewed attention to children with special needs, young people from the Roma community, and other vulnerable and marginalised groups. Health education has taken on greater significance and, since the reform of the curriculum started in 2004, there has been civic education concerned with alcohol, drugs and smoking.

Beyond compulsory education, the secondary (further) education system then splits into general education (the pathway for progression to higher education) and vocational education. Despite our observation about the appetite for learning amongst Albania's youth, the Ministry of Education reported that a major challenge was to attract young people to move beyond compulsory education into either of these forms of secondary education. It then conceded that "around 80% of students already do this"! The aspiration is for the proportion to be even greater. There are acknowledged barriers, both cultural and structural, that can prevent those who may wish to participate in post-compulsory education from doing so. For young women in particular, there can be the obstacle of traditional gender expectations. For others, it is their remote geographical location that makes progression opportunities inaccessible. It was acknowledged by the Ministry of Education that some kind of triple-track approach was probably needed to address these concerns: more contact and dialogue with families, an increase in dormitory provision and perhaps an expansion of vocational schools that could enable young people to learn a "profession" (trade). Indeed, a governmental objective is for the proportion taking a vocational route after the completion of compulsory education to rise from the current 30% to 40% by 2013. This would be a challenge, for another respondent observed that "vocational studies tend to be looked down upon, despite a lot of efforts to talk it up". The 27 professions (trades) cluster around four key sectors: agriculture, construction, mechanics and economy (culture and tourism). The development of agri-business in rural areas is of particularly pivotal importance (as the international review team learned during its visit to Bushat).

> During the 1920s there were no international aid programmes to provide Albania with the economic and technical assistance she needed to modernise and develop. The country was forced, therefore, to rely upon the assistance in various forms of private philanthropic agencies and individuals. One of the most important of these non-governmental ventures was the Albanian Vocational School in Tirana (AVS) or 'Shkolle Teknike'. ... [T]he AVS provided its students with both classroom instruction and practical experience in a broad range of vocational programmes. It operated a commercial printing press, an electric power station, an ice plant and a farm. It also undertook several construction projects. (Vickers 2008, p. 129)

The international review team was told by the Ministry of Education that, in the field of vocational education, gender issues were "not really an issue". Given the transnational gender divide in vocational learning, with boys opting for construction and mechanics and girls opting for health and social care and hairdressing, this comment took us by surprise, especially as health and social care has traditionally been located in higher educational, not vocational learning. The official in question further observed that "generally the number of girls and boys are relatively equal", though he was referring to Tirana and he did acknowledge that "the issue is more related to rural areas, where gender issues may be part of that story". For the international review team, this was confirmed in its visit to a vocational school where not one student was a young woman.

**The professional school**

The professional (vocational) school, was, however, impressive, almost worryingly impressive, for all the students appeared to be wearing brand new overalls! The international review team, hosted by the director, was shown round a sequence of workshops, with about 14 boys in each, aged between 15 and 18. Most workshops focused on electro-mechanics, with further specialisms in domestic electrics (washing machines, cookers, fridges and microwaves), commercial application and installation. We then moved on to the auto-mechanics workshop where the learners were developing not just general automotive skills but also more specialist skills relevant to agricultural machinery; the director noted that many of the students came from the countryside and so these skills were particularly useful. There was a car mechanics workshop where "third party" work was done: in other words, car repairs on a commercial basis. There was also a welding workshop, described by the director not as an alternative but as an integral part of the training. The director was also very keen to show us the ICT provision in the main building but, regrettably, we had run out of time. He also noted with pride that the staff in each workshop now had the resource of a computer and access to the Internet.

While the training offered is clearly not "primitive" it is certainly not the highly computerised approach to "car mechanics" and related occupations that has characterised training in western Europe for at least the past 20 years. Yet that would probably still be inappropriate in the context of Albania, where most of the private and commercial vehicles are relatively older (and therefore requiring older skills). As the director pointed out, the skills being learned by these boys will equip them for personal use and for use in their neighbourhoods, maybe through setting up their own small businesses. He said that in the third year, many went on placements with employers and subsequently were taken on. And as De Waal (2007, p. 138) registers,

> The acquaintance who took us to our new base was a mechanic with a large minibus acquired through a sister in Germany. Albania, now known as the graveyard for Europe's used cars was the right place for a mechanic, he told us. "Before I was making very little money indeed. With all these imported cars in very poor condition, I have as much work as I like".

The school has been supported with donations from a Swiss organisation that has also helped them to modernise their curriculum. When asked about the absence of girls, the director responded that there are currently no girls and never have been; these are not their subjects! There is a dormitory providing residential places for those who come from far away. In all, there are around 500 students. The director argued that the new ICT provision may attract girls for the first time. But there is a high demand to attend the professional school and it has a recruitment process and eligibility criteria that include not only the grades achieved through nine years of elementary schooling but also a dedicated intelligence test (though its content was not outlined).

### Education for democracy and entrepreneurship

It would be easy, but inappropriate, for the international review team to focus in on the observed gender imbalances in education, especially vocational education. This must clearly be a challenge for the future. For now, Albania faces other educational challenges, well beyond these or those of preparing young men to repair well-used Mercedes. Indeed, the Ministry of Education was forthright that its main overarching general educational challenge was "educating young people for a democratic culture, and educating them to face a market economy". These demand reforms and change at the level of educational infrastructure: the introduction of enterprise education and preparation for entrepreneurship (present in post-compulsory secondary education and higher education, but "not so obvious yet" in the compulsory school curriculum), and the inclusion of young people in structures of school governance. These are but two of a menu of generic reforms currently on the agenda of the Ministry of Education, but they are still in relatively early days. And quite rightly, it was asserted that the process could not be rushed through the uncritical adoption of models established and allegedly proven elsewhere: "We have to find ways of how to do [these things] appropriately according to our situation and our needs".

Finally, in the context of compulsory and further education, there are now both psychologists and careers counsellors in every school to support young people in these times of change and considerable uncertainty. There are dedicated rooms in each school for this purpose, and the service provides guidance both to students and to their parents. Education for careers has now become a compulsory element of the curriculum.

### Higher education

There were very mixed views about the proliferation of higher education and the high levels of participation in universities, despite the uncertain futures that the resultant qualifications often conferred. The Open Society Institute (formerly The Soros Foundation), with a dedicated labour market project in the Korca region (population approximately 350 000), was unequivocal: "it is not so much a problem with the universities, though now there are 19 private universities, but too many young people study liberal arts, economics and administration that do not directly serve the labour market". Other respondents felt that the private universities were a poor option (indeed, it was considered "better" to try and study abroad, in order to secure credible "currency" for higher educational qualifications), almost "exploiting" the demand for higher education, but there was resistance to the idea of any formal public regulation and instead a belief that, over time, the market would settle and the weakest private universities would fold. Though it was currently an unregulated private market, the average cost of private university education was around €3 000 a year, which was not considered to be "extortionate" and many argued that some of these institutions were "reasonable universities".

**Albanian students abroad**

There are currently around 25 000 Albanian students studying abroad. There is now a youth NGO dedicated to their interests and the contribution they may make to Albania in the future. It is a network representing those planning to study abroad, those currently doing so, and those who have done so in the past:

> Given that Albania is a young country, we think we can use our knowledge and experience to make a difference in this country: generating ideas, developing activities, engaging in politics, promoting issues (such as gender equality, youth and employment, environment). Our members can contribute to Albania whether or not they come back. We have been active in the drafting of the National Youth Strategy where we wanted more emphasis on young people abroad, because there was no focus on them until three years ago. Then there was the "brain gain" project, but there is still much more to do. Albanian youth are more or less everywhere. We need to get them involved: not only in the labour market but also in the drafting of policies. But there still needs to be support from the structures to "exploit" these cultural and work experiences. The desire to come back is big, but there is a need to create more bridges and channels to motivate return and to facilitate engagement and contribution. Need better governance of the local tax system, for example, and those from abroad can illustrate the pros and cons of different models. *(Albanian Students Abroad Network (AS@N))*

The Mayor of Shkodra was adamant about the importance of young people having "contact with European institutions, to exchange experience and to touch foreign realities by themselves". To that end, the region has endeavoured to create the conditions for young people to study abroad and then to return; the mayor cited four students who had studied in Florence and who now work for the municipality. When students study abroad, there are 'spin-off' benefits such as potential contact with the respective university and the Chambers of Commerce where that university is situated. Albanian students abroad, it was claimed, do not do any worse, and often do better, than other students: "we feel very proud that students from this town manage to achieve the highest standards in their graduation, especially when in competition with young people who have grown up in far more favourable circumstances".

**Minority education**

In Shkodra, too, there was a sense of achievement at having re-established a new school for Roma children. The former school had closed in the 1990s and "this had generated some problems" in that even fewer Roma children were attending school, but now the new school was providing for some 135 Roma and Egyptian young people. At the Roma community centre in Tirana, there was a clear emphasis on education at all levels: kindergarten provision, a learning room for the girls, and one for the boys, and a team of young adult volunteers whose own educational success conveyed what Roma young people can achieve. Nevertheless, just as at the Roma community centre in Shkodra, there were patent tensions between learning and eating: parents still took their kids to the streets to engage in begging, even when they knew the importance of education for those children's futures.

**Special needs education**

Sometimes names of institutions can prove to be misleading for the uninformed! At one particular moment, the international review team was under the impression it would be visiting a "social community centre" and was at first surprised, perhaps even disturbed, at the very structured depiction of its operation and activities. Slowly, however, it transpired that it was in fact what might be termed a "special school" or a "therapeutic social work centre", catering for children and young people with "limited abilities" (mental and physical disabilities). Around 150 people benefit from its services – through children attending school, sessions for parents, training for members of the community, outreach work in the community and sports and leisure programmes for young people in the afternoons – every day. The centre has been working in the community since 1997.

Once this was apparent, the international review team was impressed with the "cocktail" of services available both to the children and their families. Beyond the educational and social provision enshrined in a personalised plan, to which parents and children are contractually bound, there is a commitment to the provision of vocational training that may hold some prospect of real employment afterwards, often assisted by the networks forged over time by the institution. The centre now even offers a meal for local elderly people, often the grandparents of the children who attend the school. Children and young people (and their families) are referred from across the whole of Tirana. The institution is, no doubt, an oasis of exemplary professional practice in what is otherwise something of a desert of provision. Its experience and expertise has certainly been called upon to contribute to the preparation of drafts for legislation with regard to people with disabilities and on questions of gender equality (such as Association for Women and Children 2002). The director said that there was now more work being done elsewhere in Albania for children and young people with limited abilities and difficulties. There is, apparently, a plan to open seven other similar centres in 2010. One is nearby and just needs equipment to be installed before it can open; the others are still being built.

**Non-formal education**

Approaches to what might be called "non-formal education" will be discussed mainly in relation to our focus on leisure time. The international review team observed some embryonic thinking and understanding, especially amongst those who had experience of training in such approaches from other countries, but there was, equally, a great deal of misunderstanding, with the terminology used randomly and casually without any real sense of meaning. Within schools, there was clearly a commitment to the provision of learning beyond traditional formal academic subjects. We heard about curriculum programmes concerned with civic, health and free market education, but we did not learn much about exactly what is delivered, how it is done, who does it and how they are trained. There were also measures to teach young people about Europe. The pedagogical rationale for these programmes was to promote dialogue, change attitudes and effect behaviour change. Yet while, from an Albanian perspective, such measures may be considered "non-formal", they are probably not delivered in ways that would be recognised as "non-formal learning". One community-based initiative around the learning of English, that might fit such a definition, has been inspired in part by the desire to combat the problem of young people having nothing to do, in part to engage with different people and thereby develop social skills, and in part to learn through different methodologies from those routinely used in school. Beyond that, however, there was very little evidence of non-formal educational practice in Albania (see a longer discussion both in the section on leisure-time activities, and in the Conclusion).

The international review team broadly commends the direction of educational reform within compulsory schooling in Albania. There appears to a commitment both to reshaping a formal curriculum, creating space for more optional topics for study which can be determined by students, and inserting a "personal, social and health education" element in the curriculum, addressing issues such as drug misuse and sexual health.[8]

---

**Recommendation 1**

*The international review team acknowledges the need for a greater educational focus on economic and enterprise education,[9] but believes the Albanian authorities should think about this not simply in terms of business innovation and entrepreneurship but as a pedagogical method for promoting initiative and creativity in young people. There can be education for, through and about enterprise (see Jamieson et al. 1988, Rees and Rees 1992).*

---

The international review team was pleased to see a growing commitment to educational opportunity and provision for young people from minorities and those with special needs, though there is clearly a long way to go – current provision represents, so far, some beacons of excellence.

---

**Recommendation 2**

*The international review team is concerned at the lack of understanding of the concept and methodologies of non-formal education which could be applied more, not only in the community (as we discuss below) but also in more formal educational structures, in order to address many of the "social" questions (of health, participation and democracy) that the Albanian authorities are currently addressing.*

---

8. One observation during the national hearing was that there should be religious education in schools. The international review team felt that this might better be called moral education, addressing the values that are central and often common between many different faiths.

9. At the national hearing, one comment was that Albania needed to have more job creators and not so many job seekers.

## Vocational training and the labour market

> [B]oth professional education and professional training retain a low profile reputation among young people and older generations – insofar as the quality of the programs offered and the low percentage of students enrolled are concerned. (Ministry of Tourism, Culture, Youth and Sports 2006, p. 21)

> The current system of Education and Vocational Training (VET) (sic) in Albania is weak, quantitatively and qualitatively. In general there is a lack of proper infrastructure, insufficient funding, a low level of human resources, relatively old curricula which don't meet labour market needs and old management methods. (Ministry of Labour, Social Affairs and Equal Opportunities 2007, p. 22)

Some 20% of the total number of unemployed in Albania is between 15 and 25 years old. Indeed, around 50-60% of this age group, according to the Ministry of Labour, Social Affairs and Equal Opportunities, are not in employment, though many of them will be in universities, of which there are many private institutions.

As a result, the Sectoral Strategy on Employment and Vocational Training 2007-13 (Ministry of Labour, Social Affairs and Equal Opportunities 2007) has been developed. Though an International Labour Organization (ILO) project, it has endeavoured to synchronise with the National Youth Strategy (the time frames are the same) and sees, for example, the possibility of attaching employment services to the information services foreseen by the National Youth Strategy to be part of the regional youth centres initiative.

In response to the frequently aired concern that university graduates are not able to find work that is commensurate with their qualifications, the ministry has established a focus on graduate unemployed job-seekers and put in place a job placement process in enterprise in return for unemployment benefits for six months – in order to provide the starting experience for getting a job.[10] Though there is not yet any formal evaluation of this programme (one will be starting in 2010), professional knowledge – through the employment offices – suggests that most young people on this programme do get jobs. Currently, the programme is only for university graduates, but it is hoped that in due course something similar will be developed for those completing secondary education.

The ministry noted that "there is a big problem in that everyone wants to go to university, so there is a gap at secondary education level and corresponding labour market destinations". When the international review team raised the point about "over-qualification", the response was cautious. This was a "difficult issue". There were, anyway, questions about the validity of some of those qualifications that were claimed to be of university level: "those who graduate from [some] private universities have questionable qualifications". One NGO concurred with this perspective, but maintained that it was a clear legacy of the

---

10. At the national hearing it was pointed out that, certainly in Tirana, there was already an established tradition of collaboration between the university, the Chamber of Commerce and local business to provide job placement opportunities for university students.

communist era, when many young people did not have the opportunity to attend university. Now that they can, parents encourage them to do so. This fuels a demand, to which provision is made through a private sector, market-based, response – and the opportunity can be taken, even if the provision is not even formally accredited. In time, the NGO maintained, a different balance may be struck when young people realise that job prospects may be greater if they follow more vocational routes. A review of the Albanian framework of qualifications is currently in process.

The ministry acknowledged that there was a scenario where graduates leave university to come out and work as waiters, but they do at least have jobs. The primary focus of the ministry has to remain on those who become and remain unemployed. The guarantee of unemployment benefit (around €55 a month) provides some small incentive to take part in the "traineeship programme", as well as its reasonable promise of serving as a stepping stone to a more appropriate job.

## Strategic thinking

Despite the ubiquitous problem of having access to up-to-date data, the ministry is endeavouring to identify labour market needs, shortfalls in supply, and the means of bridging the gap between them. In time, it is argued, this will help to ensure a better "fit" between young people in Albania and available jobs (most of which are "growing" in small and medium-sized enterprises [SMEs], which comprise 85% of private companies in Albania, and so are rather difficult to engage with). The ministry is seeking to co-ordinate the efforts both of state agencies and those in the private sector in order for them "to work together for the benefit of the local market". The two main growth sectors towards which particular effort is being directed are tourism (the demand for waiters, guides and cooks – though this remains, inevitably, very seasonal and geographically specific) and construction and its related trades, where future projections are reasonably optimistic. There remains much to be done in terms of co-ordinating the many different players, at many different levels, in this particular area of youth policy: the ministry, employment offices, private agencies, private business, young people, education and training institutions and NGOs. An overarching strategic view remains very much in its infancy.

## Regional approaches

At the regional level, in Shkodra, there has been a concerted effort to employ "well-prepared and well-trained" young people in the public administration – in order to "cope with the challenges we face today". According to the mayor, producing such qualities demanded a high level of educational participation and subsequent performance and attainment. Only through the creation of such a context would a climate favourable to business development be cultivated, alongside simple procedures for investment. With some support from the ministry and also from the Italian Bank for Development, Shkodra had achieved some notable successes in attracting several foreign companies and promoting the establishment of micro-businesses. There are plans to have a business school in Shkodra to support the growth of the private sector, and this will be advanced in collaboration with the Chamber of Commerce and the University of Torino.

### Brain gain

One initiative[11] of some significance has been the "brain gain" programme, encouraging young people to return from abroad. It has been running for four years and there is quite a high demand for internships both in the public and private sectors.[12] One public university has already attracted professors back from elsewhere. There is also a subsidy programme for those returning to work in the public administration. The issues regarding those returning from abroad are complex, and one respondent summarised them admirably:

> There is the challenge of making use of their [vocational] training from another country and then the challenge of their re-integration in the labour market in Albania. We have worked on these aspects but it is difficult. If they come back to open a business here, what we wish to do, if they have learned particular skills abroad, is to make use of those skills more broadly. But it is difficult to motivate these people to make that contribution that we would like from them. And then there are the challenges of engaging with those who have been unsuccessful when they have been abroad. If they couldn't make it in an open labour market, then it will be even harder for them to make it here. Further to this there is a project that is about establishing a centre of excellence in Tirana so that we can then expand the idea to other regions of Albania.

This will, no doubt, be easier said than done, particularly as the project mentioned at the end of this quotation, which has been financed by the Italian government (and supported by the ILO and latterly the International Organization for Migration, or IOM) has been in the process of development for the past eight years. Not that Albania is short of ideas. Indeed, one youth NGO, the Idea Institute, has as its explicit *raison d'être* the development of ideas, especially for the youth of Albania. It consists of young professionals who have graduated both in Albania and abroad and who now want to contribute "to thinking about how this country

---

11.   Though the international review team was not informed about it during the review process, feedback from the ministry drew attention to a Joint Programme of the United Nations System in Albania that started in January 2009. Focused on youth employment and migration, the programme has been developed in co-operation with the Ministry of Labour, Social Issues and Equal Opportunities, the Ministry of Youth, INSTAT, business organisations, trade unions, youth organisations, local government and international organisations such as ILO, IOM, UNDP and UNICEF. The Ministry of Youth has played a key role as a facilitator of the process, developing evidence-based policy making, and serving as an implementation partner. The international review team was surprised that it had not learned of this particular initiative earlier.

12.   At the national hearing, a representative of the Albanian Students Abroad Network (AS@N), which had pioneered the internship process in Albania, argued that what was needed in addition was the opportunity for Albanian students studying abroad to have the opportunity of internships within the European institutions in Brussels and Strasbourg.

should develop". It addresses different processes of social life, particularly the ubiquitous challenge of employment and questions about education, especially in relation to Bologna issues. Similarly, those students who are part of the Albanian Students Abroad Network ( AS@N ) are contributing to new forms of thinking gleaned and adapted from their many experiences abroad. Amongst many commitments, it seeks to strike an improved balanced between private enterprise and private ownership, and public intervention and regulation. To avoid "the Wild West", the prospect of European integration is a great asset as it provides appropriate illustrations of laws and regulations that can become models for business governance in Albania.[13] But it has not happened yet! However, there is an Albanian saying that "when you are fulfilled, you have nothing to dream of"!

> The international review team sees considerable potential in the new vocational education strategy and applauds its progressive and realistic thinking. There will, however, always be challenges in trying to establish "parity" between that and academic education. It has never been achieved elsewhere, whatever the labour market benefits of following that route.

---

***Recommendation 3***

*The international review team sees many merits in the "brain gain" programme, both to encourage the return of Albanian young people studying abroad and to establish career pathways for educated young people within the public administration. Such intellectual leadership may be required, but care should be taken to avoid strengthening what may be perceived as an already relatively privileged elite in whom disproportionate public resources are invested.*

---

## Health

> Albania was included in the EHCI at the request of the Albanian Ministry of Health. "We might well finish last, but we want to be in there anyway", the ministry wrote in an email to the researchers. But it did not come last. Of the 31 countries surveyed by the Brussels-based Swedish think tank Health Consumer Powerhouse, which produced the European healthcare consumer index, Romania and Bulgaria came below Albania. (*The Budapest Times,* 5-11 October 2009)

Writing about the Hoxha years, Vickers (2008, p. 199) is complimentary about developments in health:

> Some notable improvements were also made in the field of health care, with free medical treatment available for all. Hospitals, clinics and sanatoria were built, and the average life expectancy increased from 54 years in 1950 to 67 years by 1970.

The international review team was extremely impressed with the vision and described practice conveyed by senior officials within the Ministry of Health. It was, however, concerned that there appeared to be relatively little collaboration

---

13. Indeed, the ministry was keen to emphasise that many of Albania's recent laws and regulations have been drafted on the basis of European Union models.

with the Youth Department and relatively little connection with the National Youth Strategy, although the Ministry of Health had contributed to the formulation of the strategy (on matters such as sexual reproductive health, where an action plan established by the Ministry of Health was about to be disseminated to other ministries). There appeared to be closer links with the Ministry of Education in relation to school-based health programmes. Unlike other respondents, who were often apologetic about the proliferation of strategies and action plans (but still no action!), the Ministry of Health was quite unapologetic. It argued the case and need for ensuring the involvement of a range of stakeholders "within the health sector and beyond" including, significantly, the NGO sector (in particular the international UN agencies such as UNICEF and the United Nations Fund for Population Activities, or UNFPA) and the Ministry of Education. As one official put it crisply:

> We would see that it is important to integrate primary health care and public health services, and to build youth-related health activity onto existing services around our centres for testing and treatment.

### Youth-focused and friendly measures

To this end, there are aspirations to develop the 12 existing regional centres that have been established (with the support of the Global Fund) to test for HIV/Aids in order to expand them into more youth-friendly health services. Now that one aspect of recent reforms has been the regionalisation of public health services, there is even more commitment to strengthening this sector. There are already five youth-friendly health centres (which have been developed with the support of UNICEF, though they are unequivocally health-led rather than informed by wider youth services), and specialists for public health and dedicated children's workers concentrating on health education and promotion. In Tirana, there is one school physician for at least two schools and they are also involved in doing health promotion. For the first time, following a reorganisation of primary health care services (there are 420 primary health care centres in Albania), one performance indicator is health promotion, with a focus on sexual and reproductive health. The essential problem is the stigma young people claim to experience if they attend public services, resorting instead, as a result, to private – and sometimes illegal – sector provision for both contraception and abortion, with the concomitant risks (and costs) that this entails.

### A role for NGOs

The ministry supports NGOs to take on health interventions with young people on the street, particularly around substance misuse and sexually transmitted infections, including HIV/Aids. It was conceded that "hard-to-reach" young people – those from the Roma community, street kids, sex workers and drug users – represented a "delicate problem". The ministry acknowledged that it probably did not have the formal structures to meet the needs of these groups but it was determined to keep services for them in mind: hence the engagement of NGOs to carry out the delivery of those services for them. One of the most prominent of those NGOs is Aksion Plus, which contributed to the drugs and public health section of the National Youth Strategy, and delivers the methadone maintenance programme mentioned above. It also provides counselling and advice to drug users and to young people depicted as "MARA" (most at-risk adolescents) and education and advice services for parents. Aksion Plus has cultivated strong political contacts and is clearly a key player from the NGO sector not only in delivery but also in shaping strategy in the health field.

## School-based initiatives

The ministry felt one of its significant achievements, through collaboration with the Ministry of Education and with the support of UNFPA, had been the production of a very good health education curriculum with a central focus on reproductive health that would be delivered by school psychologists (see above), school doctors and teachers. Aksion Plus also contributes to this. Indeed, from most corners of health policy, there was a consistent celebration of the quality of collaboration and co-operation, commitment to innovation and modernisation, and recognition that a range of approaches is required.

## Substance misuse

There is a modern, creative approach to addressing the challenges of serious drug use, though its prevalence (as far as can be determined, and gauging usage accurately is always fraught with difficulty) is relatively limited in Albania. HIV is not evident amongst intravenous drug users (but questions were raised about the methodology of the research that drew this conclusion), though there is considerable evidence of Hepatitis C (one estimate has put it at 27% of the injecting drug population). It was suggested that there are about 200 clients at the methadone maintenance centre in Tirana (there are three such centres in Albania, and a residential rehabilitation centre run by a religious community). Indeed, around half of the Global Fund budget is committed to harm reduction practice, notably methadone maintenance and needle exchanges. There are balances to be struck, not only within the health policy field between primary, secondary and tertiary prevention, but also between health promotion and treatment and law enforcement. Albania, it was noted, is a transit country for drugs. The debate remains, however, largely restricted to a focus on heroin and cannabis use. There is limited attention to emergent issues such as the misuse of over-the-counter and prescription drugs, or Internet-accessed "legal highs" (such as GHB and GBL). Similarly, practice development has not yet embraced new wisdom around brief intervention and motivational interviewing, although a Balkan network is being developed to address such questions. Nevertheless, Aksion Plus, the only NGO of significance in the field of substance misuse, is confident about Albania's direction of travel in this field:

> Aksion Plus is the only NGO that is working in this area and it is slowly promoting thinking and awareness, in different ways, across those who work in various sectors: such as high schools, prisons. We are working beyond our capacities to support the wider mechanisms, including parents. We cover a range of activity: advice, information, training, interventions, debate. I see myself as in the middle of a wheel of activity, working within the realities, whatever the politics and the prejudices.

## Sexual health

At a more general level with regard to health issues and young people, there has been a lot of attention paid to family planning services, through private pharmacies, social marketing (the supply of pills to private retail outlets) and the 420 primary health care centres. Yet there appears to be limited use by young people of "modern" contraceptives. It was suggested that "the target for many young women is early pregnancy". For those for whom it is not, there is apparently a reluctance to use publicly-established services (such as those above) allegedly because of concerns about anonymity, stigma and confidentiality. Instead young people use private clinics for abortions, or emergency contraception from pharmacists.

## Alcohol and smoking

The scale of alcohol and tobacco use by young people, particularly those under the age of 18, is also a source of concern and new measures and laws have recently been introduced addressing issues such as sales, use and advertising. The recent study by the Albanian Association of Psychologists (2008) suggests that over half of young people (aged between 13 and 35 years) are regular smokers and a quarter of these smoke more than 20 cigarettes a day. Four fifths have consumed alcohol in the past 12 months, though one fifth has never drank alcohol. Yet, despite strategies and action plans to reduce the prevalence of both smoking and drinking, there has been limited success in enforcement. The use of tobacco in bars and restaurants, despite a smoking ban, continues to very publicly flaunt the legislation. With alcohol, there is a lot of use of home-made alcohol and the ministry is adamant that it needs more robust data – on things such as lifestyle profiles, time of day, place of use – in order to decide on the most effective and appropriate policy approach. Health issues are clearly prominent in the minds of at least some young people: the international review team was impressed at the work on this front (on smoking and drugs) being done by the Youth Parliament in Durrës.

## Mental health

One area where the international review team was as concerned as the Ministry of Health was around the mental health challenges facing young people. It is well established that psycho-social disorders in young people tend to escalate in times of social dislocation (Rutter and Smith 1994); Albania's context is one that is very likely to produce the anxieties and uncertainties that fuel mental ill-health. The ministry accepted that it might well be a challenge but that there was little data on the issue. Nor was there much anecdotal evidence, such as the reporting of violence in schools. Not that the ministry was complacent: it had introduced mental health issues into the training curricula for school psychologists and school doctors and it was also part of the training of some teachers. Mental health remains a delicate matter to broach: "we have inherited a culture of not discussing this aspect of health because mental illness was previously considered to be a very bad thing". The ministry is eager to introduce modern protocols (such as community mental health centres) and, in time, will do so. Currently it is more concerned with consolidating its role and influence on a health agenda for young people that previously had been largely carried out under the auspices of the UN agencies. It is eager to forge a more coherent approach, one that is "less scattered amongst different activities". To put everything in context and to avoid getting too carried away with a specifically youth-focused health agenda, the ministry noted that the resources committed to public health through the law on public health have been allocated to two priorities viewed as guaranteeing a basic public health platform for the people of Albania: disease control and water sanitation.

### The knowledge base[14]

There appear to be general concerns about the reliability of data on key health matters. Albania is not, for example, yet part of the European Monitoring Centre for Drugs and Drug Addiction (EMCDDA)'s coverage on drug addiction. The data on substance abuse presented in the National Youth Strategy (Ministry of Culture, Tourism, Youth and Sports 2006, p. 28) is drawn from the public order system, not from health research. The Institute of Public Health says that 60% of young people in school have smoked marijuana. One of our respondents was convinced that "the drugs issue in Albania is very big", though in high schools it was mainly smokeable substances (tobacco and cannabis). The costs of drugs, it was argued, were certainly not prohibitive for teenagers. There is, nonetheless, no reliable baseline data on these issues (a parliamentarian conceded that there was insufficient monitoring of drug use) and other analysts have also suggested that Albania in fact has a western European profile for substance misuse (Albanian Association of Psychologists 2008). Moreover, as borders open up and visa restrictions are lifted, in relation to both HIV/Aids and drug use, the returning population may become a significant issue.

### Gaps in provision

Despite all these proclaimed and apparent advances in thinking and practice in relation to specific health policy challenges, the international review team encountered some worrying issues in relation to general health care and a fundamental absence of "decent health structures". At a community centre in Shkodra, it was reported that infections and diseases were widespread, with limited access to health services. Few individuals had health insurance because they were not in work; moreover, their addresses were "not really" recognised because they lived in what are known as "informal areas" (see below). If people do not have health insurance, they have to pay for any health care, including vaccinations. It was put to the international review team that it was perhaps a

---

14. During the national hearing more than one respondent argued that there were statistical and other research data available, especially in the health field, but they maintained that "what we need is a system that analyses and presents these data in a useful way". This is the challenge when the position is, arguably, 'data rich but information poor' – material has to be distilled to ensure policy usefulness and relevance.

surprise that there was no doctor and no nurse in the area. Given that the majority of these people were Roma and Egyptians (native, but more dark-skinned Albanians), this was considered to constitute a "lack of respect and discrimination against our people", one that affected the life-chances of their children from a very early age "because they don't really have any decent conditions for growing up". At least at the Roma community centre in Tirana, there is a regular visit from a nurse who gives some time for free "but sometimes needs to be paid". We were told, however, that the hospital, where health care can be accessed, is not so far away.

---

### Recommendation 4

*Though impressed with the technical thinking of those in the health field, the international review team was concerned that health strategies are largely divorced from some of the wider social and economic realities of young people's lives, which require more incorporation and focus if effective health strategies are to be developed and implemented. There were glimpses of such thinking, such as at the SOS Kinderdörfer International Children's Village, where medical support for families and their children is part of the package of intervention that helps children to remain with their families, or assists them in returning to them.*

---

### Recommendation 5

*The international review team would have liked to have learned more about the capacity of street-based NGOs to refer clients to more mainstream, state-funded service provision.*

---

Given the limited discussion of mental health issues amongst young people in Albania, the international review team was somewhat perplexed about the provision of psychologists in every school and wondered whether these were more focused on educational guidance, counselling and the resolution of school-based issues rather than providing attention to wider mental health problems.

---

### Recommendation 6

*Researching "invisible" populations always, inevitably, presents methodological challenges, but a stronger evidence base on drug use, sexually transmitted infections, and the prevalence of HIV/Aids in Albania would seem to be urgently required.*

---

The progressive vision for public health conveyed to the international review team in Tirana, does not seem to translate into practice – certainly not yet – for many people in Albania. Access to basic health care would still appear to be an issue for some. This should be a source of concern for a country seeking candidature for the European Union.

## Housing

> The trajectory of change has been clear enough. Thanks to emigrant remittances, life inside most flats and some rural houses has become more comfortable with the acquisition of new sofa beds, television, washing machines, fridges, electric cookers and radiators. (De Waal 2007, p. 14)

Housing has often been an overlooked and neglected dimension of youth policy, despite the increasing pressures on available and affordable independent living for young people across Europe. Albania, especially Tirana, appears to be no exception. What is different from some other parts of Europe is the apparent acceptance by parents that their children may continue to live with them up to the age of around 30. This is, indeed, part of Albanian tradition – even if it has now become too expensive to do otherwise in Tirana.

### Dormitory provision

The international review team learned relatively little in detail about the housing circumstances of young people. There is a students' town in Tirana, with separate provision for males and females. Accommodation there costs around € 300 a year, in comparison to a small apartment that would cost around € 200 a month, or a room at around € 100-150. (A "not proper" job in Tirana would apparently pay some € 300 a month, "though a waiter might earn more".) The international review team recognised the importance of dormitory provision for students both within and beyond the capital city. Indeed, it observed such facilities at the professional school in Durrës, and welcomed those aspects of the vocational training plan that signal the intention to provide more dormitory provision to ensure access to vocational training for young people from rural areas.

### Informal areas

The international review team was less able to make full sense of conditions in what were routinely described as "informal areas", though it understood that these were, at least initially, illegal settlements adjacent to the cities and the coastal plain constructed by internal migrants from more remote rural areas. It was also sometimes a term for the anarchic development of housing on property that was not clearly identified as belonging to anyone in particular. De Waal (2007, p. 137) observed their early development:

> To the north of Tirana, there was now a growing number of wooden shacks erected by northern villagers ... The government at this period [late 1990s] was wisely letting them stand. Given that Albanian cities were very small under communism thanks to the policy of rural population retention, there was plenty of scope for urban expansion. The extremely serious housing shortage in Tirana might as well be alleviated by self-help as by a bankrupt government.

Those we spoke to from both Tirana and Shkodra maintained that living in such "informal areas" had (negative) implications for provision such as schooling and health care. Yet, though there remain questions of ownership, compensation and other things and though, of course, there is not the infrastructure that would have normally accompanied more planned development, we were told that at least some of the "informal areas" were now in a process of legalisation, a point also noted by De Waal (2007, p. 237):

> Shortly before the 1996 election, changes occurred on this part of the plan [near Durrës] altering the status of two groups. The squatters, who had mostly been squatting since 1992 and had no "passportisation" rights, were granted *pasaportizimi* in a bid by the Democratic government to secure their votes. Thereafter, these squatters were recognised administratively as living in the *komuna*, with the voting rights, access to birth and death registration, schooling for their children, etc. which this entails.

These "informal areas" were not dissimilar to the kinds of spontaneously developed shanty towns that can be found the world over. Clearly, young people growing up in such environments have certain limitations on their own development. As a result, the international review team recognised the importance of the "space" afforded through, for example, the Roma community centres in both Tirana and Shkodra. For young adults who desire to live independently, however, some thought might be given to innovative housing strategies that allow for self-build, redesign of existing apartment blocks and shared part-rental and ownership – in order to support this particular element of transitions to adulthood. Housing, in the National Youth Strategy (as in most youth strategies), is conspicuous only by its absence.

---

**Recommendation 7**

*Housing issues for young people are likely, in the relatively near future, to become a critical youth policy challenge. Dormitory provision will almost certainly not be enough, however important it may be today. Some creative thinking – perhaps around conversion of dilapidated buildings through vocational training initiatives, or even self-build schemes – is urgently needed.*

---

## Family

"My parents teach me that the most important thing is to work and make money." (dropout boy, aged 12)

"Trust is the most important value, because if parents would not trust their children, there can't be harmony between them." (high-school girl, aged 16, Fier)

"Our parents think that behaviour of young people has deteriorated, this is why we have conflicts with parents. Of course we are more bold in what we do. We have more choices." (high-school boy, aged 16, Tirana)

(Institute for Development of Research and Alternatives 2008, p. 150)

Most children have "very good" or "good" relations with parents. Among most frequently mentioned reasons for good relations were the communication, love and care that the parent showed (Institute for Development of Research and Alternatives 2008). The vast majority of children and young people live with their immediate or extended families, until and often beyond the time they get married. The average age of marriage is now around 26, and the first child follows soon afterwards:

> So there is now some delay compared to previous times. This is perhaps because of studying abroad, living independently and trying to make a living, and also, these days, young women can make more autonomous decisions than before. Before, they did what their families expected them to do.

Working women can take maternity leave for a year with an income of around 60-70% of their former wage. Working women who have children do tend to continue working. There is no paternity leave.

A parliamentarian reported that "there is still a tradition of strong families in Albania, which can be very positive around education and culture". Indeed, parents appear to be very committed to the education of their children (often because they themselves did not have the same possibilities), and tolerant and engaged with wider opportunities for, and interventions with, their children (such as sexual health education). There are, of course, significant variations, especially between families in more urban and more rural areas, the latter being predictably rather more conservative. Yet, even in Bushat, the most remote area visited by the international review team, the young people we met displayed considerable occupational ambition despite the fact that many said their fathers had relatively humble jobs and their mothers were "'housewives" (though they no doubt did a considerable amount of unpaid work).

The international review team was interested in two particular phenomena: young people growing up in precarious family environments and requiring some level of "public care", and those who are caught within traditional blood feud antagonisms.

### Children in need of public care

The SOS Kinderdörfer International leaflet on *Preparation for Independent Living* notes forcefully:

> International studies show that young people who have been in care are more likely to be undereducated, unemployed or underemployed, homeless, or even to be living below the poverty line. They are more likely to become young parents, to be dependent on social assistance, and have higher risks of mental illness and substance misuse.

It might have added some of the additional risks of becoming entangled with the criminal justice system or subjected to abuse, exploitation and trafficking. The international review team learned relatively little about state support for neglected or abandoned children. It had a brief meeting with officials in the Ministry of Social Affairs and was told of the state's objectives to support young people who are orphans, with social problems and families in difficulty. There have been reforms since the early 1990s and a recent sectoral strategy on social protection for 2007-13. We were informed in general terms of the National Strategy for Children 2005-10 and other measures for groups in need, including children: those with disabilities, those trafficked or at risk of trafficking, abused children, Roma and Egyptian children, and children who beg. Though we sought some detail about concrete measures, we were generally informed of the technical and bureaucratic infrastructure: the many "technical secretariats" and liaison officers responsible for monitoring developments and reporting to inter-ministerial committees headed by the deputy prime minister.

The international review team was given some rather more concrete detail on domestic violence within families (a law was passed in 2008 and various measures adopted, and there are plans to establish a national centre for abused people). It also learned of the recent development of four regional and 10 municipal child protection units, staffed by social workers and responding to referrals from schools and the community. For children requiring residential services, these are provided both by the state and by NGOs. There used to be 26 state-run residential centres, but there has been a process of decentralisation and now 19 are the responsibility of municipalities. There are seven dedicated residential centres for different groups in need (for children up to the age of 3 in Tirana, 4-6 year-olds in Shkodra, an orphanage in Tirana, and centres for the victims of trafficking in Tirana, disabled people, old people and children involved in blood feuds) and one, mentioned above, that is planned for the victims of domestic violence. Those NGOs providing social services for different groups are now regulated by a National Licensing Centre and standards are ensured by an autonomous inspectorate. So, without ever really grasping the actual nature of provision, the international review team was told that "the triangle is complete: NGO provision, government standards and inspectorate". It could have been argued that the picture should in fact have been one of a square, incorporating issues of accessibility and availability for service users!

> The international review team became increasingly concerned about the absence of concrete illustrations of practical interventions in the lives of children and young people, rather than detailed descriptions of legislative intent and governmental infrastructure.

Where the international review team did secure a stronger grasp of what can be done for more disadvantaged and neglected children was during a visit to the "Children's Village" to the south-east of Tirana. Run by SOS Kinderdörfer International, it provides for 80 children in a variety of ways and through a range of overlapping and interlinking objectives. Reminiscent of classical British "cottage homes", children aged up to the age of 14 live in groups of seven in 13 dedicated housing units run by "housemothers". The project does everything it can to support the retention of children in their families through offering guidance and assistance to parents (a programme started in 2003, extended in 2006 and consolidated in collaboration with other service providers and municipalities in 2007) but, if necessary, it takes the child away from the family and attempts to "replace" the parents, especially through the provision of surrogate fathers. The state social services make referrals and then the SOS village has an admission committee to assess need and decide on response. SOS Kinderdörfer International can refuse children, but they would not refuse siblings. They are unable to cater for children with physical or learning disabilities. The Children's Village only takes children up to the age of 10, unless they are siblings of children who are already there.

The international review team was told that state support for children stops at the age of 14, though we received different information. Young people are required to leave institutional care at the age of 16, but if they stay at high school they live in dormitories. Orphans aged between 18 and 25 who are without work do receive state benefits. There are also some priorities in employment policies and vocational training for these groups. They get more help with scholarships, and are the focus of efforts to forge links with the business community (we were provided with the example of a mobile phone company funding 20 scholarships). But it was conceded that it was still a challenge and a problem to make appropriate provision for that particular group of young people at that particular age.

In contrast, the SOS Children's Village, Albania, now provides help to young people up to the age of 26. Its "youth work" – primarily for young people aged between 14 and 18 years old – started in 2001 when the first SOS young people moved to rented flats in Tirana. At the beginning of 2005 a larger flat was purchased in order to meet the increasing need for accommodation for SOS young people (www.sos-childrensvillages.org/Where-we-help/Europe/Albania). Beyond the Children's Village itself, then, this NGO provides a kindergarten, a school, two social centres (operating a "Family Strengthening Programme"), the youth facility (mentioned above) and a vocational training centre for young people over the age of 14. The SOS Leaving Care project, which runs from 2009 to 2011, seeks to bring together learning and understanding from all its projects across Europe with the aim of improving knowledge sharing, promoting youth participation and empowerment, and bringing about change in legislation and practice.

---

**Recommendation 8**

*The international review team was impressed with the work and innovation of SOS Kinderdörfer International, though it wondered how much of the "iceberg" of need its work really penetrated. Its significant message, nevertheless, is that with appropriate support, young people who are disconnected from their families can achieve in education, find suitable and secure employment, live in stable housing arrangements, and build productive relationships. This is an important lesson for the government, which should encourage it to consider extending the age range across which it supports young people who have formerly been in need of public care.*

### A blood feud family

Throughout the 20th century the different administrations of an independent Albania sought to rid the country of its ancient tradition, particularly in the north, of blood feuds:

> The new constitution of December 1928 gave Zogu unrestricted legislative, judicial and executive powers which extended to his personal dictatorship. The enforcement of law and order was seen as an essential prerequisite to the progress of the country. Zogu thus decreed the abolition of blood feuds. ... (Vickers 2008, p.123)

Referring to the government reforms in the 1940s, De Waal (2007, p. 79) notes:

> On the positive side, blood feud was more or less eradicated by the end of the 1950s thanks to new laws and severe sentences ...

Yet such proscription and prohibition was clearly ineffective, simply driving time-honoured traditions underground, from where they surfaced as soon as the draconian regime of Hoxha had passed:

> [B]y the spring of 1996 there were an estimated 60 000 people actively involved in blood feuds throughout northern Albania, leading to 900 vendetta-related deaths that year. (Vickers 2008, p. 241)

The bases of such disputes were many, not always to do with physical violation and the drawing of blood but on account of land disputes and other family rivalries. And, in the absence of the effective rule of "modern" law during the 1990s, recourse to more traditional forms of dispute resolution, based on what is known as the Kanun, was commonplace (see below). The *komuna* of Bushat was therefore proud to report that today "things have got so much better, and no pupil has to stay at home and miss education because of blood feud issues". The mayor spoke of having managed to resolve one long-standing dispute and reconcile two families. The international review team was privileged to be able to pay a visit to one of these families to learn directly what the implications of blood feuds can be for children and young people.

After a warm welcome and the sharing of raki, the patriarch of the family told the story. There had been a dispute with someone in the same village:

> After the dispute and both sides being very angry, one from that family was killed by us. For the past 15 years we have tried to get involved in a process that might resolve this dispute, so that peace will reign once again. The other family was eventually of the same opinion, after the continued efforts of many people – people with authority in the community and the Catholic and Muslim leaders. The local population also helped but the most significant were the Chief of the Commune and the police directorate of Shkodra, as well as the faith group leaders.

It is interesting that strong reference is made to the role of faith group leaders, despite the proclaimed insignificance of religion in public life in Albania. De Waal (2007) notes that it is as much the strength of personality of individuals who may just happen to be faith leaders as any status invested in them because of their religious role. She suggests that, following the abolition of religion in 1967, religious orders were still sometimes able to prevent the re-opening of a blood feud, though "successes were due to the force of personality and eloquence rather than to any religious conviction on the part of listeners ... the Kanun carried far more weight than church laws" (De Waal 2007, p. 79).

The reconciliation had taken place earlier in the year (2009). It was explained that, in blood feuds, all men can be targets, but women should not be touched under any circumstances. This meant that a child in the family, a boy now aged 14, had been a possible target of the blood feud, from a very young age, though assurances had been given that he would not be touched for two years, until he could walk. For that reason he did not attend kindergarten, for his own safety, but after that he was accompanied to school by members of his family, in order to protect him. The school authorities also provided support and protection; it was customary law that the school should be a safe environment, though there were times when things got very difficult and the boy could not attend lessons, during which times teachers came to his home to help him keep up with his learning. The international review team was told that he was only likely to be vulnerable if he was alone, and "so he was never left alone". It was also mentioned that although revenge on young male children was a legitimate course of action within blood feud traditions, it has generally not been applied recently, so even though the family took great care in protecting the boy, the risks for him were probably less than those in relation to the adult men in the family.

The resolution of this particular blood feud has become something of a *cause célèbre* in the region. It has paved the way for a reduction in blood feuds; although some are still going on, none now involve children. A new project in Shkodra called "second chances" involves teachers, psychologists and social workers following up the children who were previously involved in blood feud issues, about 34 children in all.

> The sustaining of "blood feud" traditions in modern Albania provides a salutary lesson that if the rule of law, and respect for it, cannot be secured, the people will look elsewhere for guidance and for "justice" (and sometimes retribution). In northern Albania, there continues to be reference to the Kanun of Leka Dukagjini. That blood feud disputes can be resolved is also instructive: the personal capacities for forgiveness and peace-making, the contribution of respected figures in the community, and the increasing penetration of the rule of law. Things remain fragile. The international review team was simply grateful for the opportunity to hear an account of this cultural phenomenon first-hand from a family that had been at the centre of it.

## Religion, culture, tradition and values

There is a recent book on Christianity and Islam in the United Kingdom that suggests that some forms of faith, irrespective of the particular faith, contribute to community cohesion while more fundamentalist versions of the same faith can actively or passively produce community division (Billings 2008). Despite former attempts to create the world's first atheist country, religion in Albania appears to be a force for the good, performing – as the international review team was told on a number of occasions – "more of a social than a spiritual role". In Bushat, it was proclaimed that "the inter-religious situation is very good". In all places we visited, religion was not viewed as an area of conflict, despite the reasonably significant presence of three faith groups (Muslim, Catholic and Orthodox). We were told that it is not an obstacle for people of different faiths to marry, nor to youth engagement with sex education, where parents were often grateful for such interventions. Though religion did not necessary enhance social ties and functioning, neither did it impede them.

There are, however, some caveats and contradictions to this very positive perspective. Within the general context of tolerance, openness and secularity, there were the inevitable contrasts between approaches and attitudes in Tirana and other cities, and more rural areas, where religion made at least some contribution to patriarchal social arrangements and gender divisions. Girls were "married off" at the age of 15, and there had to be separate provision for boys and girls when a youth NGO was eager to develop language courses in one rural community. Even in Tirana, there were different rooms for girls and boys at the Roma community centre, allegedly to establish a "safe space" for the girls but equally as a gesture of respect to particular cultural traditions rooted in faith perspectives. However, the international review team was told that these kinds of traditions were rapidly diminishing and becoming "remnants" of the past. New role models were being established, such as those of the educated young woman running the Roma community centre in Tirana: parents see the value of departing from traditional norms if modern opportunities are to be conferred on their children. Nonetheless, the role of faith leaders as "go-betweens" and as the agents for reducing antagonisms was still considered to be very important in the blood feud situations in the north, largely because of the respect commanded by the individuals who held those faith positions. The contribution of faith leaders to the resolution of the dispute involving the blood feud family we visited (see above) was emphasised by officials of the municipality, the school directors and, indeed, the patriarch of the family itself.

---

### Recommendation 9

*Given the very unique religious traditions in Albania, there is enormous potential for faith groups to make a contribution to the "social" sphere within which young people are growing up. The international review team had only glimpses of this potential – from remarks made by respondents, and from the role of faith leaders in the resolution of the blood feud dispute – but feels that more consideration should be given to it.*

---

## Mobility/migration and internationalism

> The two commonest survival strategies since the end of communism have been migration abroad and descent from mountain villages to plains and plains towns. At least two thirds of the households from the villages I got to know have left. (De Waal 2007, p. 241)

There are, inevitably, some "big issues" regarding mobility and internationalism on the part of young people. Over the period of the first seven Council of Europe international reviews of national youth policies (1997-2001), mobility was generally considered only in a positive light: young people had opportunities to travel and study abroad. Subsequent reviews, however, drew increased attention to what might be called "negative mobility" – the movement of young people through trafficking for sex purposes, or through exploitation for the purposes of unskilled and often illegal labour. Albania has its mix of both positive and negative international mobility, with a significant number of young people studying abroad (despite the fact that travel remains obstructed to western Europe because of visa requirements, though these are about to become more relaxed), but also deep concerns about trafficking, especially of young women.

### Internal migration and population retention

Albania also has issues concerning internal migration. Since 1990, there has been a significant re-distribution of the population, with districts in the north decreasing in numbers, while the Tirana and Durrës districts experiencing considerable demographic growth.

> In an attempt to escape unemployment, poverty and the alarming increase in blood-feud killings related to arguments over the redistribution of land, thousands of northerners migrated southwards leaving many mountain communities virtually abandoned. ... The government could do little to stem the migration of northerners to Tirana and the resulting growth of the shanty towns into permanent suburbs. ... (Vickers 2008, p. 241)

While Hoxha had enforced an urban-rural equalisation programme, this had anyway had limited success (De Waal 2007, p. 96) and during the early 1990s, there was a dramatic exodus from the more remote rural areas. This was probably exacerbated by the absence of any apparent regional development strategy, an issue that concerned the international review team before it was confirmed in reading De Waal (2007), who comments at different points:

> Regional development, still less decentralisation of decision-making, were not even under serious discussion until the end of the decade. (p. 85)

> It was two or three years [after the end of communism] before disillusionment set in with the realisation that regional development was not part of the government's program and that out-migration was the only solution to economic survival. (p. 99)

Central government's lack of interest in or commitment to regional development, like its neglect of agriculture generally, has been a major obstacle to economic progress in Albania over the past decade. Where progress depends on government institutions, advances are hard to find. (p. 245)

The international review team had in fact asked the Ministry of Social Affairs about the issue of a rural economic development strategy to counter internal migration trends. The answer was forthright and blunt:

The reality is that it is extremely difficult to live in those areas. They have poor agricultural land, and no possibilities of tourism ... Hoxha tried to keep people in the countryside. Albania is no longer trying ... though the Prime Minister has been discussing this: a social inclusion strategy, a development and integration strategy, the role of the Ministry of Agriculture ... And the National Migration study did look at which areas had been most affected by out-migration.

The Youth Ministry also admitted that "we are not doing much in this field". This was because of other priorities (ironically related to the issue of internal migration) such as congested schools in Tirana. The Ministry said that even after high school and university study in Tirana, young people from other regions often wanted to stay in the capital, though "if they cannot get a job that they want, some of them go back". Part of the National Youth Strategy is the creation and development of regional youth centres and there was hope that "with the new centres there can be more support for young people staying and young people returning". Partners Albania, a youth NGO, was already trying to cover the 12 regions of Albania, "although in some remote areas we still can hardly talk about civil society and activism". Nevertheless, it has tried to work with high school directors and those in youth organisations to support local initiatives (with very limited funding – around US$1 000 a project), and felt that it had detected "small aspects of local change".

It was therefore refreshing to discover the commitment being made in Bushat to a broad-based, co-financed social and environmental development plan, incorporating attention to infrastructure such as the management of waste, the provision of piped water, the cleaning up of rivers, and the conservation of flora and fauna (see Bushat Commune 2008) but also very pertinent youth-related issues such as schooling and leisure-time provision. A new school has recently been constructed that "has been a solution to the education problems in that village" and there is also a farmers' school located in the district, though this is a national facility. Attention has been paid to the high schools and to the provision of sports fields, supported by the municipal budget and additional funding from donors and the state education budget. De Waal (2007, p. 244) notes that poorly functioning education is a "significant factor" in provincial out-migration, so we should commend the commitment of Bushat to this area of youth policy, even if, ultimately, it may be driven by self-interest. It would appear that there is no longer an inclination to "let the market decide" and to be more proactive in addressing questions of population retention and return. Hence, for example, the rural touristic plan in the north, designed to produce jobs and a reason for staying. Given that we learned in Fier that 80% of those who study elsewhere do not come back (the two who ran the youth centre had done so "for personal reasons"), these are important developments.

In Bushat again, prospective population retention was being supported by improved use of agricultural land (the mayor said that the "entire agricultural land is now in use") and more collective enterprise. These can be difficult ideas, given the particularities of Albania's political history, as De Waal (2007, p. 89) points out:

> Initially, an extreme concept of privatisation, an understandable reaction to excessive collectivisation, resulted in rejection by some individuals of any notion of community rights or common good.

Surprisingly, this is despite the Kanun's tenet that public good overrides private gain. Those memories, however, are now being superseded by a more economic rationality and the recognition that small units of land, the product of Albanian traditions of inheritance, are never going to be competitively productive. One of the individuals observing the meeting between the international review team and local dignitaries, young people and residents was a farmer who told us with confidence and self-belief that:

> In the village where I live, we have established the first co-operative of the farmers dealing with covered agricultural areas. We've had support from the Spanish government: the number of people in the villages who are working in agriculture is increasing. It is economic collective action now, which was resented and resisted a few years ago because of our history.

### Travelling abroad

When the international review team spoke to young people in Tirana, Durrës, Fier, Shkodra and Bushat, many were asked whether they had ever travelled abroad. Many had done so, though usually for holidays or on school trips, and to neighbouring countries such as Italy, Greece, Montenegro, the former Yugoslav Republic of Macedonia and Kosovo. One had been to Turkey and one of the youth workers, a facilitator of a youth parliament, had been to Sweden for training on youth engagement, entrepreneurship, youth policy and women's issues. This appeared to be quite typical for some groups of young people: young people of school age had tended to travel more "locally" while youth NGO leaders had travelled and trained in more distant countries. Only one of the Roma young people we met in Shkodra, however, had ever been out of Shkodra – and that was for a hospital visit to Tirana. And not one of the young people we met in Bushat had ever been abroad.

### Studying abroad

Not very many of the school-age young people said they had aspirations to study abroad, though those who did appeared to be very determined to do so. There does appear to be an almost disproportionate focus on those who do study abroad, though these individuals are, of course, those who can potentially bring back a distinctive body of expertise and experience to improve the social and economic situation of Albania. The National Migration Strategy does not in fact have a dedicated youth section though there are various measures that refer to the phenomenon of "brain drain" and the facilitation of those who return to Albania. Furthermore, in 2008, the Ministry of Labour had become a partner in a project with the Ministry of Social Affairs on the migration of young people – how to benefit from this migration and how to lower risks. This is a governmental project implemented by the UN and financed by the Spanish government. It is concerned with building the capacity of local employment institutions, establishing co-ordinating mechanisms to facilitate the integration of young people and supporting the "brain gain" programme. A further objective is to connect young people with the Albanian diaspora and work with the diaspora so that those who have graduated abroad will return to Albania. Emigration and immigration (return) continue to be seen largely as individual decisions, though the Ministry of Labour is currently working on drafting a study on those who would like to return and how the institutions in Albania meet their needs – whether in terms of work, language needs (for the children of returning people) and other issues.

The "brain gain" programme is a major plank of youth policy in Albania. Referred to in the National Youth Strategy (pp. 19-25), it seeks to address the barriers to students returning from abroad: the lack of information concerning job opportunities and career development potential. The programme is strongly supported by the AS@N, which has obviously lobbied for it and contributed to its development. There was little consensus, however, about the reasons why well-qualified young people might want to come back, other than that it was for a range of different reasons. Some, of course, had always planned to return. Another youth NGO, the European Youth Parliament, has also "imported" expertise and understanding from other young people across Europe and, indeed, held its first Albanian based international meeting in Durrës at the end of November 2009. These, and other youth NGOs providing for the needs and interests of students and an intellectual elite, were constantly critical of the barriers to mobility presented by the visa requirements in relation to the European Union, though, with a new accord, these have very recently been relaxed and the situation is likely to improve further as Albania becomes closer to the Union.

### Youth programmes abroad

A final aspect of youth mobility is the European Commission's Youth in Action programme. To the astonishment of the international review team, the Ministry of Integration (responsible for establishing compliance with the *acquis communautaire*) appeared to have absolutely no understanding of Albania's role in the Youth in Action programme. Indeed, we were told that "so far" it had "no record" of any applications. The ministry had apparently invited young people to a session to inform them about the programme, and about 60 had attended, "but we don't know what the outcome was". It also appeared to be quite oblivious of the National Youth Strategy until a second official told us that there was a Strategy for Youth and offered to arrange a meeting for the international review team with the Ministry of Culture! Given that Chapter 6 of the National Youth Strategy is about Albanian youth as future European citizens, we were quite incredulous that there was such a poverty of knowledge, especially given the recurrent claims about cross-ministry structures that facilitated co-operation and communication.

The Youth in Action programme is, of course, a major contributor to the making and shaping of "European citizens". In another of our meetings, we discovered one youth NGO[15] that had been involved in the programme since 2006 and "we even spread the news about that European Union programme to other youth NGOs". Some individuals had attended a European citizenship course (it was not clear whether this derived from the European Union or from the Council of Europe). There had been attendance at a European Voluntary Service promotion earlier in 2009 about how to work with volunteers and the process of "sending" and "hosting", though "we have only sent so far". The international review team did not learn exactly how many young people had been involved in the programme, nor in precisely what way – but it was relieved that there was at least awareness of it and some engagement, for youth exchange and mobility has always been the guiding and governing *raison d'être* of the European Commission's youth programmes ever since their inception around the time Albania emerged from communism.

---

**Recommendation 10**

*The international review team had serious concerns about the apparent absence of any regional economic development strategy in Albania. The out-migration of young people from more remote and rural communities is a common feature of many countries, but it is possible to think about "growth centre" strategies, in the interests of social, cultural and economic "rescue", if rural communities are not to suffer from demographic imbalance and ultimately die out.*

---

The international review team welcomes the relaxation of visa regulations for young people who may wish to travel or study abroad, notably in Europe. This will bring benefits not only to the individuals concerned but also to the broadening of horizons, experiences and expectations within Albanian youth culture more generally.

The international review team recognised the importance of transforming the recent "brain drain" into a "brain gain" through supporting Albanian young people who went abroad in returning to Albania. However, we have expressed some caveats to this important programme in a comment under Vocational Training and the Labour Market above.

---

15. Of course this was not the only youth organisation to benefit from the Youth in Action programme. In its feedback, the ministry provided a list of those which have currently applied for funding through the programme, on themes such as intercultural learning, European citizenship, inter-religious dialogue, the empowerment of young people from minorities, youth participation and the European Voluntary Service programme.

## Minorities

The international review team witnessed some impressive commitment to "minorities" which is, of course, part of Albania's noble tradition (during the Second World War, not one Jewish person was betrayed to the Nazis – instead they were given new identities and hidden in the mountains). Yet this should not cloud the fact that there was also a palpable difference between the "mainstream" Albanian population and the Roma people in particular – in terms of the conditions of their lives, their opportunities, their experiences and their perspectives. Explaining the reasons for this is clearly beyond the scope of this review; what should be given careful consideration is how to build on some of the positive developments we heard about and saw and how to address some of the concerns that we also had.

Since the end of communism, there has apparently been a Roma strategy, which endorses the integration of the Roma people into Albanian society, but – as with many governmental strategies – there was a pervasive feeling that little practical had been done. Nevertheless, one senior member of a Roma community did comment that "We feel lucky to be living in Albania, given the situation of Roma in some other parts of the world, and I don't want to hand down my pessimism to the younger generation. We must be optimistic". He had some cause to be optimistic, given our experience of the Roma community centre in Tirana, where educated young Roma are contributing in a variety of ways to its provision.

There does appear to be some confusion about exactly what projects and provision are trying to achieve with regard to the Roma minority. In Shkodra, the (re-)establishment of a Roma school was mentioned with some pride, as was a partnership forged between the Roma community there and that in Tivat in Montenegro. But elsewhere, there was a stronger commitment to bringing the Roma and non-Roma communities together, especially young people. In Fier, around a fifth of the participants at a recent summer school were Roma and the remark made by one of the youth workers is instructive: "Following participation, they are more like part of us; people started not recognising them as part of the Roma community". The youth centre in Fier endeavours to involve Roma young people at various levels, through programmes such as peer education, health education and drugs prevention. "We try to adapt ourselves to accommodate the particularities of the Roma", said one of the youth workers.

There was mention of "all different but equal", though not explicitly linked to the Council of Europe's campaign (2006-07) on human rights, democracy and participation. The goal amongst other projects was certainly to celebrate the strengths of Roma traditions and culture but to do this in the context of all Albanian youth, not as some exotic "show" based on stereotypes about the Roma and dance and music. Roma young people could also succeed in education and community involvement. There was an equal determination to co-operate with non-Roma organisations and work with non-Roma young people to break down stereotypes of the Roma (such as not knowing how to work and not wanting to do so) as well as helping to change the mentality of the Roma by broadening their horizons. This was something of a contrast to other contexts, where the prevailing position remained one of complaint and dependency, and an expectation that others should be doing more for the Roma. Self-help, however, cannot usually take place in complete isolation, and the progressive and committed approach observed by the international review team in Tirana was supported by funding from the Swedish government. Indeed, it was noted that where the Roma were "moving forward" it was largely helped by international donors rather than through any domestic support.

There are always inherent tensions – which exist everywhere – in the debate about the relationships between majority and minority communities. The western European position of multiculturalism, which itself took many years to evolve, has now been called into question in some quarters. The broader debate is evident, though rarely made explicit, in Albania. People seem unclear as to whether they are advocating assimilation, integration, acceptance or acculturation (for an early discussion of these questions, see Banton 1972). There were certainly stark differences between those who, for example, supported the establishment of separate schools for Roma youth, those who wanted to strengthen access to mainstream education for Roma youth, and those who wanted to construct an educational offer to Roma young people building on the realities of Roma life-worlds and a moral stand concerning their entitlement to education.

Perhaps more practically, the international review team was very conscious of the apparent absence of young people from minority ethnic groups (including Roma youth) within youth structures. Though we asked time and again if and how representation was secured amongst young people who, for whatever reasons, were not in school, we received rather tentative replies. A more concerted effort to hear the voice of "minority" youth is probably required. This applies not just to ethnic minorities, but also to sexual minorities, about whom we learned nothing. This appears to still be a rather taboo subject in Albania. There may be many awareness campaigns around access, inclusion and equal opportunities, but nothing specifically on the question of sexual orientation (despite the reports of the prime minister saying he would like to see same-sex marriage on the statute book by the end of the year, though this was dismissed by some as a public relations stunt). Nor was there any mention of national minorities, language minorities or other ethnic minorities: Greek, Macedonian, Montenegrin and others who are perhaps even less easily identified. This may be because there are few relevant issues rather than, as can be the case in other countries, a product of a convenient amnesia. Finally, when asking about the "Egyptians" (who are often spoken of in the same breath as the Roma), the international review team was informed that they are a people of darker skin but who speak Albanian and therefore they cannot be considered a national minority because they speak the same language. This is an interesting and unusual distinction, which might well not resonate in other countries.

> **Recommendation 11**
>
> *The international review team felt that, despite the Albanian people's generally tolerant attitudes and particular history in relation to minorities, various minorities remain excluded from even the policy dialogue and others are subjected to considerable rhetoric but apparently limited intervention. Across a range of policy domains, more targeted and concerted efforts seem to be required.*

## Volunteering and "social" work

In the discussion of families (above) we make some reference to social services provision by both the state institutions and the NGO sector. Here the international review team is more concerned with the "social" work conducted by a range of youth and other NGOs across a range of issues. In the context of Albania, just as in many other places, this energy and effort is significantly a product of people giving free time to projects and activities. Such "volunteering" carries very different meanings in different parts of Europe (see Williamson et al. 2005), yet since the European Union White Paper on Youth (European Commission 2002) "voluntary activities" have been a pivotal dimension of youth policy discussion.

The international review team met large numbers of volunteers and, whatever the reasons for making such commitment, the work carried out could not possibly have happened without them. It has, however, been a "struggle" to promote the idea of voluntarism because, in the past, the concept had not really existed though "doing things for nothing" had been a requirement under communism. One respondent commented:

> Talk of voluntarism has particular meanings here, because in the past people were forced to do voluntarism. It is a dirty word. And anyway most people need to work, earn money and support families. So voluntarism is a privileged position and opportunity.

As a result, especially given the culture shift to a rather rampant capitalism in which making money is now the dominant individual goal for most Albanians, the idea of giving time for nothing, for the benefit of others, is often considered tantamount to crass stupidity. Speaking of the perceived lack of penetration of the National Youth Strategy beyond Tirana, another respondent was asked what might be done and commented on the value of volunteering:

> A small step is bringing young people from Tirana to see what is going on in the countryside and to contribute to things like the international camps. They often think that being a "volunteer" is being stupid, because of past cultural expectations, so you have to try to persuade them of a role that maybe they do not think of as working as a volunteer. But in this way, both sides change because they see different realities from both sides.

The essential characteristics of "volunteerism" (or volunteering or voluntarism) are outlined by Gjeka (2009, p. 15) in a study of the perceptions and realities of volunteerism in the Albanian Youth Sector:

- it is undertaken of one's own free will;
- it brings benefits to a third party as well as to the individual;
- it is not undertaken primarily for financial gain.

This is a far cry from the reasons why volunteerism often has negative connotations still, because under the period of communist dictatorship "it was the first punishment in the black list of consequences for dissidents of the regime" (Gjeka 2009, p. 17). Gjeka points out that this so-called volunteerism was also used as a means of building the infrastructure of Albania, from the construction of bridges, railroads, factories, schools, roads, terraces, drainage systems, tunnels to the building of prisons and bunkers. However, Gjeka emphasises that there can be two perspectives even on "volunteerism" during that period: a negative interpretation, that it was a way of cutting costs and enslaving the people and a more positive interpretation, that it was a solution to the problems of an underdeveloped country destroyed by conflict over many centuries.

There are good reasons to re-appraise the idea of volunteering, drawing both on present needs and other parts of history. Indeed, the Kanun of Leka Dukagjini provides illustrations of voluntary help and involvement; volunteering is thus embedded in Albanian tradition, culture and society and an important contributor to the development of citizenship and civic engagement and the formation of social bonds and networks. It is also a means of bringing young people together, something noted as especially necessary for Albania in a recent European Youth Forum (2007) report following a study visit to Albania.

Three fifths of young people surveyed in Gjeka's (2009) study said they had been involved in volunteering, in many different ways and for many different reasons. Respondents in that study also identified a considerable number of obstacles that impeded or inhibited participation in volunteering. These included (Gjeka 2009, pp. 33-35):

- lack of information on volunteering opportunities;
- lack of organisation of voluntary activities;
- insufficient motivation and sensitisation;
- lack of knowledge of the (potential) benefits of volunteerism;
- family and social education;
- public perceptions on volunteering (prejudices and mentality);
- time constraints;
- indifference, interest in (more) entertaining activities;
- economic situation – the need to earn a living;
- lack of credentials and incentives recognised by the state.

None of these are unique to Albania, though their balance and impact may be different. Thus there is a strong case for a concerted effort at a number of levels to change perceptions about volunteering and to improve the support and recognition of those young people who choose to become involved in volunteering. The international review team was told by NGOs that there are plans to introduce a law on volunteering "because we don't have one yet, and there is considerable support for that". At the youth centre in Fier, volunteerism was promoted in all the activities it did. One of the youth workers had in fact written her thesis on the subject (Motivation in Voluntarism). It was argued that through the new school curricula voluntarism would be promoted at even earlier ages and "as a result, there will be impressive changes in our country. We know that our previous generations hated voluntarism because it was practically mandatory. That is going to change". The youth centre in Fier has in fact organised campaigns in schools to discuss and promote (amongst other things) voluntary activity. Indeed, though there are undoubted obstacles to volunteering (not least the need for people to earn a living), some of which may be eased through legislation and attitudinal change through education and experience, the international review team was reminded constantly just how much a dedicated band of volunteers is already giving to the country, particularly in relation to key youth policy issues such as youth participation, leisure time and health. The passion and commitment they display towards the issues on which they are focused is something to be deeply admired.

> **Recommendation 12**
>
> *The international review team recommends that greater efforts are made in legislation and education to develop a better understanding of and commitment to the idea of making a voluntary commitment to the "social" needs of others, especially more isolated, marginalised and disadvantaged young people.*

## Gender equality

We have already remarked briefly about gender equality and the clear differences between public rhetoric and private realities, as well as those between urban and more rural contexts. In principle, especially within the educated milieu, there is clearly not an issue, though in practice women have not yet normally achieved equal or even the designated proportionate representation at the higher levels of, for example, politics or education (30% of the parliament are meant to be women, but to date the percentage is only 15%, though that is progress on the past). And there was a strong consensus that gender issues are not as significant in Tirana as they are in more rural parts of the country. One female NGO leader, talking of initiatives taken in more rural areas, said that during a summer camp there was a cultural expectation that boys would be the "boss"; moreover, she said that she was often not taken seriously by families, because she is a woman. In politics, the international review team was told on more than one occasion that, although there were now some women who were prominent in national politics, there remained a cultural view that women cannot – perhaps should not – take decisions that are of national importance.

Within the NGO sector and indeed at the level of youth participation, however, it was generally the boys and the men who were missing, even when "constitutionally" youth parliaments such as that in Durrës required two vice presidents from each of the sexes. In Bushat, we asked where the boys were and the girls present replied that they were playing sports! The girls in Durrës who expressed some desire to be politicians said that they lacked role models and therefore motivation, though they also felt that they could achieve their ambitions if they really wanted to. (There is in fact a network for female politicians called Woman to Woman, which is supported by a Swedish NGO.)

If the principle and philosophy of gender equality is to translate into concrete action, nowhere is this better illustrated than in the work of youth NGOs, where there is a huge over-representation of women leaders. Elsewhere in Albanian society, the situation is less promising, though there is undoubted progress, and in fields such as vocational education, more proactive measures are arguably required – a kind of "you can do this too, if you really want to" approach – if fairly entrenched cultural stereotypes are to be challenged and broken down.

---

**Recommendation 13**

*The international review team commends the explicit formal position on gender equality and the areas where this is clearly also a reality. However, it believes that in some areas and sectors of activity, a more proactive strategy is required to challenge prevailing traditions, assumptions and stereotypes.*

---

## Young people with disabilities[16]

The international review team was told that there were many organisations doing work on disability in Albania. Regrettably, though, they tend to fight only for the rights of their particular target group (which may be defined by age or by type

---

16.   Young people with "limited abilities", and the issues that affected their lives, were a major focus of debate during the national hearing. There were claims that the law, based on some relevant studies, is sufficient to produce inclusion for those with limited abilities, particularly with regard to those attending universities. Mention was made of the steady shift from residential to community services. Another respondent noted that there was the possibility for young people with disabilities to access professional and vocational training through the eight regional centres and the mobile team in more remote areas. Later in the national hearing, another individual who worked with young people with disabilities noted that some 3-4% of the Albanian population have some form of "limited ability" and she felt that a priority was more contact between young people both with and without disabilities.

of disability). As a result, "there are lots of divisions across the disability sector". For this reason, one NGO, Beyond the Barriers, has established an association trying to link those with disabilities and those without. It reported that there was not a great deal of prejudice, perhaps because of the preparatory work undertaken by the organisation.

Life for young people with disabilities was considered to be very hard, a legacy from former times "when a medical model prevailed". Public buildings, including schools and universities, were simply not accessible to those with a range of physical disabilities. Now there were attempts to promote a social model of disability, based on the idea that access is a function of the built environment, not the physical impairment of individuals. It remains difficult to get dedicated funding for turning the idea of the social model into practice – such as establishing access to bookstores (the one in the centre of Tirana requires the negotiation of a large number of uneven and often broken steps, rendering it impossible for wheelchair access and hazardous for those with other motor difficulties). The government does give a payment for people with disabilities that might allow for broader participation, but most still remain at home because venturing out remains extremely hazardous. Some people with disabilities attend special facilities, and there is an institution in Tirana for 6- to 18-year-olds with learning disabilities (this, we believe, is the community social centre, or "special school" we visited). At the SOS Kinderdörfer International Children's Village, mention was made of a centre for autistic children.

Gradually, there has been a shift in perspectives on disability, from the traditional "medical" model to a more contemporary "social" model, which was reflected in the laws regarding new buildings (requiring lifts and ramps), but unfortunately such laws were often not respected (a point which attracted general consensus amongst our respondents at that meeting, was that many laws are not implemented but are simply ignored).

Given the number of campaigns, seminars at the local level and indeed research on Roma young people with disabilities, as well as the support provided by the Open Society Institute (Soros) for projects focused on people with disabilities, it was surprising that this "category" of young people hardly gets a mention in the National Youth Strategy. At strategic points throughout Tirana, there is a very obvious public visibility of disability, with amputees, blind people and others begging on street corners. Different views were expressed to the international review team about this but, nevertheless, disability appears to be a widespread phenomenon in Albania, from which few individuals can claim complete disconnection and therefore one might have imagined the issue would have been more of a governmental challenge, rather than one simply left to the commitment of a range of NGOs.

> The international review team was interested in the strategic focus on disability, including young people, in relation to public participation, education and employment, especially now that a "social" model was the framework informing current legislative and policy development.

## Social inclusion, hard-to-reach young people and equal opportunities

There are clearly many young people in Albania who would fall into some general understanding of constituting the "socially excluded". The young people encountered by the international review team were often, though certainly not always, reasonably advantaged in the sense they were engaged with education and lived in traditional family structures. They were generally quite optimistic and positive about their situation and their futures.

Once more it is difficult to distinguish between the rhetoric of inclusion (see, for example, Association for Women and Children 2002) and the more grounded realities of young people's lives. The international review team understands that there is currently a law on equal opportunities being developed through the Ministry of Labour, Social Affairs and Equal Opportunities, though we were not appraised of its likely content. There are certainly some commendable strands of action that contribute to the social inclusion and support of different groups. The school's support for the boy at the centre of a blood feud (see above) is one example. The certification of educational achievement by young offenders in custody, without the stamp of the prison (see below) is another. So is the positive action directly towards young people who have studied abroad and decided to return, the relationship between the government and NGOs on health behaviours amongst excluded groups and the impressive work of both the SOS Kinderdörfer International Children's Village and the community social centre (special school) in Kombinat.

There are, however, some counter-sides to these initiatives. Rather than viewing many of them as typical of professional practice in Albania, one might, more sceptically, regard them as beacons of excellence, serving a lucky few or privileged minority very well but overlooking a wider population with similar difficulties and circumstances. There are, for example, 277 children at the SOS school, but only 60 from the SOS village: is the situation of the others really any better, even if it is quite understandable that priority is given to the SOS children from the village. If the community social centre in Kombinat in fact serves children from the whole of Tirana, how many young people with special needs do not have the opportunity of attending the school? Positive action towards students returning from abroad may inadvertently disadvantage young people who have studied inside Albania. These are classical social policy questions regarding intended and unintended consequences, and they merit reflection and discussion.

Youth policy, like all public policy, has to make tough decisions about where to allocate its energy and resources. Rarely does any economy have sufficient resources to tackle all the social issues it faces. Yet sometimes there is a risk that a concentrated focus on certain groups or issues can have the effect of further excluding those within these categories who are not reached, or disadvantaged groups beyond these categories who have not been afforded priority attention. The international review team was concerned that, despite the beacons of excellence it encountered that were certainly contributing to improving the life chances of those taking part and advancing their social inclusion, the reach and coverage of such measures remain limited.

> **Recommendation 14**
>
> *The international review team felt that more robust research is required to detect what kinds of proportions of those considered to require "social inclusion" are served by current state and NGO initiatives and the degree to which some "flagship" measures have the potential to be emulated with other groups, in other parts of the country, or on different issues.*

## The environment

"Laws should be tougher for environmental issues. There should be persons to monitor the environment. If a citizen throws trash in the street, he should be fined as in other countries." (high-school girl, aged 17, Shkodra)

"People throw trash everywhere. They think 'If others throw it, why shouldn't I?' They do not understand how much damage they do to the country." (compulsory-school girl, aged 14, Korca)

Throughout Europe, issues relating to the environment have become more prominent in the consciousness of young people as well as on more political agendas. Raising awareness of environmental issues has become a core item of youth policy in many countries, as much as campaigning on environmental issues has seized the imagination of many young people and the NGOs that have emerged as a result. Albania is no exception to these trends and, arguably, in greater need of environmental awareness, given the scarring of the landscape and the pollution created in the days of communism. According to children and young people consulted in a recent survey (Institute for Development of Research and Alternatives 2008, p. 220), high air pollution (65%), poor waste management (46%) and lack of green spaces (33%) are the most common environmental problems in Albania; children and young people say their role would be to discard rubbish in appropriate places (61%), maintain cleanliness (48%) and plant trees (36%). One of the abiding memories of Albania is, indeed, the ubiquitous domestic and industrial rubbish, strewn everywhere and dumped seemingly at random. The Local Environmental Action Plan for Bushat (Bushat Commune 2008) shows just how widespread the challenge is. Its agenda, already mentioned briefly, covers waste management, water supply and sewage, street lighting, drainage, soil erosion, the burning of forests (with drastic consequences for wildlife), damage to the growth of medicinal plants, combating the use of poisons, the maintenance of roads, the creation of green spaces, the forestation of the Mountain of Zefjane to counteract the decline in mountain climbing, dealing with the pollution of the River Drin to restore its ecosystem, and the establishment of sports grounds and playgrounds for children and young people.

Children and young people themselves appear to be acutely aware of the environmental destruction of their country. Environmental awareness is a key focus of much municipal youth activity. In Fier, for example, young people identified three key issues which they felt should inform the elections on 28 June. They produced a poster capturing the issues: the pollution of the River Gjanica, youth unemployment and the desire for a sports stadium. In Fier, too, young people (including those from the Roma community, though without identifying them as such) were involved in cleaning up the beaches. Similarly, the Youth Parliament in Durrës said that one of its main activities has been to collect signatures for a petition against building plans in Porto Romano that many believe will damage the environment.

There is growing awareness that Albania needs to strike a balance between trying to put right the environmental destruction from the past and forging an effective economic and industrial environment in the present. There is also agreement that the current "environment" – broadly conceived – is hardly conducive either to business investment, professional mobility, or tourism. That young people are concerned about these issues is heartening and those concerns should be supported and channelled into strategic action.[17] The international review team heard little about any overarching approach to environmental challenges and things seem to have been left to individual, unco-ordinated initiatives. Something rather more systematic is required. This is well mapped out in the National Youth Strategy (pp. 37-40) which talks about the development of environmental education and the involvement of young people in shaping environmental policies and programmes. These, and other policy ideas, are laudable objectives but, rather like the term "sustainable development" itself, there is a risk that broad visions fail to translate into meaningful practice.

17. At the national hearing it was suggested that environmental education should be a core part of the school curriculum. The young woman advocating this said that "everyone should think more green" and that "change starts with young people". She produced a small black bag, the product of one youth environmental project, with the slogan, in green, "Go Green or Go Home"!

# 3. Government-identified issues

## The law

> "Discipline without freedom is tyranny; freedom without discipline is anarchy – you have to find a path between the two." (President Julius Nyrere of Tanzania)

> "I asked whether they had known about the Kanun during communism when even talk of it was supposedly banned, or had they only become familiar with it since 1991. They said they had known about it all their lives." (De Waal 2007)

Throughout the time the international review team spent in Albania, it heard recurrent criticism and concerns about "the law", or – more to the point – the proliferation of legislation but a general disregard for it and limited probability that it would be implemented effectively or enforced. There are two aspects of "the law" that seem relevant to this international review of youth policy in Albania. The first is the general legal context in Albania and the general social consequences of this situation. The second is the specific effect these circumstances can have on youth policy.

### The general context

There was a general view that "without law, little will happen". The converse might also have been argued: even with law, little may happen. Notwithstanding such sweeping propositions, there is little doubt that, in comparison to the somewhat anarchic conditions that prevailed immediately after the fall of communism, Albania is now a much more ordered society governed by the rule of law. In that earlier period, it was the traditional mores of the Kanun that took over in many communities in the absence of workable or credible law, as De Waal (2007) notes:

> As long as the state law lacked force and failed to cover all the legal post-co-operative contingencies, the Kanun provided a workable, indeed indispensible framework for village authority, filling a dangerous vacuum. ... The implementation of those parts of the Kanun which deal with dispute settlement, property division and rights of way, was an important practical means of dealing with the existing legal hiatus. Adherence to the Kanun as a symbol of identity and guide to behaviour might, it

was hoped, act as a cohesive force in a society whose official ideological basis and practice of half a century had been discredited almost overnight. ... This was important because not only were central government's powers weak, its interest in areas outside the capital were very limited. (p. 85)

But his father and Tom pointed out that as long as the new government's laws either don't function properly or don't even cover some of the new situations, the Kanun is much better than nothing. (p. 119)

Using the Kanun was both an ideological assertion that pre-communist laws were better, and a practical attempt to cope with the legal vacuum since the end of communism. (p. 131)[18]

These were, indeed, the kinds of arguments invoked by the patriarch in the blood feud family in Shkodra, and others said forthrightly that if the leadership of the country failed to show due respect for the law, why should others? This was the primary cause of the reversion to the canonical approaches that have produced, *inter alia*, blood feuds in the past.

The words "respect" and "trust" had an almost umbilical attachment to any discussion of the law. There had been no respect or trust in the past and, if there was to be compliance in the future, there had to be greater levels of trust and respect. There was a need, one respondent said, "for a coherent body of legislation that is respected and followed, and discouragement of further production of laws in relation to which there is no compliance, and which just add further to a muddled and confusing legislative jigsaw." There was therefore the twin problem of an apparent obsession with producing legislation, strategies and action plans, while at the same time struggling to attract belief that they would really make any difference. There is certainly more confidence today in the law than prevailed only a few years ago, but people still remain tentative and sceptical about its authority and impact. On more than one occasion, the international review team heard of property development that destroyed Albania's cultural heritage or traditional open spaces, in direct contravention of a range of quite explicit legislation. For these reasons, trust is still in short supply, but there does appear to be growing confidence in the law. One of the professionals who accompanied the international review team to visit the family that had been involved in a blood feud corroborated this perspective:

What I can foresee for the future is that more and more trust is given to the authorities by the population, and that the challenge is to eradicate this cultural phenomenon. The more people trust more in the state authorities, the more they will also trust the way these resolve problems, rather than more traditional cultural arrangements.

One of the family members echoed this view: "If the government has punished the person with the wrong approach, then people often think things are too soft and feel that they have to do it in a way they understand better". But, despite

---

18.  Kanuni i Lekë Dukagjinit (Kanun of Lekë Dukagjini).

making that observation, the family is now wholly supportive of more concerted efforts to put an end to blood feud disputes through strengthening the authority of both national and local government in relation to the issues that have historically produced them.

The lack of credibility attached to so much legislation was not just a source of criticism by many outside the government but was also acknowledged internally, within the administration and even by the parliamentarians who make the law. There was, however, a conviction that Albania needed to be governed by the rule of law and that, despite the current challenges (one politician said "Our laws meet the standards and criteria, we are dynamic in the legal framework,[19] but there are still huge challenges in the enforcement and implementation of the law") young people needed to know what the laws are "so that this knowledge is embedded in the basic culture". Current honest intentions to improve the legislative framework remained tarred by knowledge of the flouting of the law and corruption within it, especially by the powerful, in the recent past. Nevertheless, some credit was given to current legislative processes and its content. One international NGO commented:

> In general the issue is the lack of accountability on the part of the politicians. They sometimes adopt a very easy approach when it comes to drafting their laws, strategies and plans, but when it comes to implementation it becomes another story. A lot is more of a kind of orientation or a wish-list, which is not a bad thing in itself, rather than a map with clear stepping stones and review procedures to consider progress and action.

This remark is in itself a stepping stone to the following section, which considers "delivery" in more detail, and clearly the two issues are completely intertwined. Another NGO charitably commended the production of a range of laws and action plans and said that they "looked as if they were going in the right direction":

> But then you look at the turnover of politicians and these political realities tend to "fog out" good intentions and things get left behind.

The law was disconnected from social life, which was one of the reasons for implementation problems. There was a lack of transparency and too much "knee jerk" policy development (premised on the desire to "have another law") that produced a "jungle of confusion". Some respondents could not even tell the international review team whether the budgets they described were in euros, dollars or leke (the Albanian currency) – some rather important distinctions!

---

19.  In an informal meeting with a parliamentarian after the national hearing, the international review team was told of a parliamentary sub-committee responsible for youth issues, the fact that the drafting of law in relation to young people (such as laws concerning smoking and the permissible age for drinking alcohol) was informed by round table discussions with young people, and that there were plans to introduce some form of "civic education" to help young people understand the importance and role of the legislative process.

Ultimately, those whom we spoke to argued the case for greater respect for the law and civic responsibility: "there is not much more we can do – it is part of the wider case for change in Albanian culture". Enforcement of the law certainly needed to be more robust, but more critically it had to be accompanied by a stronger belief in the rule of law and respect for its intentions.

## The law and youth policy

During the second visit to Albania by the international review team, it was informed by the Youth Ministry that there is an intention to produce a legal code on the rights of young people, youth representation and youth working conditions. This sounds promising, for the prevailing view to date is that the legal context is "not enabling" for the development and delivery of youth policy. There was a view amongst many youth NGOs that the youth sector in general is "shrinking", which is causing concern amongst donors who view it as an anti-democratic trend if civil society is diminishing. The absence of a National Youth Council (very recently in the process of resurrection) was often cited as one illustration that "there are not the national bodies there used to be". International donor interest in Albania was simultaneously declining, as their commitments were refocused elsewhere. The youth NGO sector understood that "these donors cannot fund forever" but, though Albania is moving closer to the European Union, "alternative routes of support are still difficult to determine" and legal obstacles are a disincentive to international donor funding. Philanthropy from the private sector is still not cultural practice in Albania and so the youth NGO sector has constantly engaged in advocacy work to improve the legal context for its work.

The international review team struggled to make full sense of this context. It listened to recurrent complaints from youth NGOs about the complexity and barriers around regulations governing the registration and taxation of NGOs. One respondent commented:

> The original legislative and fiscal framework was a good idea because it was a way of controlling profit-making outfits that were masquerading as not-for-profit organisations. But it is killing youth NGOs.

Another youth NGO respondent elaborated on the issue in an even more forthright manner:

> Youth is said to be a priority area. The ministry needs to be a stronger catalyst for youth policy. European funds for Albania are diminishing and being redirected towards FYROM [the former Yugoslav Republic of Macedonia] and Serbia. So, yes, we are closer to the integration process but we still need to be supported now, more than ever. For NGOs, the fiscal legislation has still not changed. There were some NGOs that were the favourite focus of donors; they took over the donations and other NGOs went down. Then there was greater monitoring of youth NGOs and so now we are treated like small businesses: balance sheets, income tax, import tax. We are caught up with the problem of fiscal evasion (no invoices), and so we have to pay more tax (because of missing invoices) than we should have to do. We are getting suffocated by the law.

The ministry retorted that attention would be given to many of these concerns in a new action plan focusing on the National Youth Strategy and stressed that "every year there is communication to the legislature about extending greater support for youth NGOs". This was met with a wry smile from some of the youth NGOs present, who pressed for "good governance" and more "enabling legislation for NGOs". The international review team invited youth NGOs to provide more concrete illustrations of how legislation impeded their operation and also invited the ministry to set out the regulatory framework for youth NGOs. Unfortunately, neither side responded to this offer. We feel therefore that we cannot make any forceful recommendation on the matter. As the international review team understands things, there is an issue that NGOs are now treated as businesses and therefore liable for the flat rate of 20% tax: "the tax system is incomprehensible and complex; the laws are perhaps made to kill the independent NGOs and to 'open' their own. It is all really problematic". NGOs are also frustrated that the government is preoccupied with legal frameworks that are often ignored, rather than supporting operation and delivery. Here we would simply like to encourage some thinking about a question once asked in the Australian youth NGO context: "Are youth NGOs the heads of a movement or the arms of the state?" One respondent summed up the dilemma that is always faced by NGOs and national youth councils: "The old National Youth Council fought with the government and got destroyed. Another model is working with the government, but then you end up talking the same language and you may as well be working for them".

The international review team further understands, from the Youth Ministry's perspective that registration as an NGO is not particularly onerous and should become even less complex when a planned National Youth Centre is established:

> They apply to the court for registration; the ministry just keeps a database of those that are registered. We are working towards the establishment of a National Youth Centre and regional youth centres that will hopefully be able to register NGOs instead of the courts. For the ministry to have formal links with the regional youth centres there needs to be a National Youth Centre which can implement the structures from the government/ministry to the regions and local communities. We have to prepare a structure for the short and long term and so there is a need for this level and mechanism – from next January [2010]. The National Youth Centre will have responsibilities for employment, information and other "youth issues". The idea was first proposed in 2008 but the last minister was not so supportive of it. The new minister wishes to get it approved. Originally it was going to be called the National Youth Agency but the name was changed because of Albania wishing to be part of the European Union and the European Union's terminology of "national agencies" for its Youth in Action programme.

The youth NGOs had different perspectives on such proposed developments; they had encountered such aspirations before and treated them with a "pinch of salt". One NGO was direct in its opinion of the current situation, of future intentions, and of what it considered to be desirable developments to support the youth NGO sector. It mentioned a proposed civil society fund through which the state would support the NGO sector.[20] A board comprising representatives from both government and civil society will make decisions on the allocation of these funds. However, like too much in the past, there has been limited transparency on the detailed proposals around this idea, which is expected to be operational within two years,[21] and it was described as having stimulated a big debate, though one that was "mostly not public". The fund would support scholarships, seminars and projects, but it was reported to the international review team by a number of respondents that there is little trust in the way the idea has been developed, the "space for political manipulation is still very great", and "the whole process would have benefited from greater consultation, democracy and transparency".

With regard to providing a more conducive environment for youth NGOs, this particular NGO offered the following recommendations:

> The state is not here to create NGOs. That has to be bottom up, but the government has to establish an enabling legal framework. This needs to have four key elements. First of all the tax regime treats the NGO sector as a for-profit business sector. It needs to recognise a not-for-profit sector. Second, there needs to be support for philanthropy through the tax system. We could emulate the Hungarian model.[22] Only sport, art and printing are supported here. Third, there is the issue of reporting relations with the government: frequency and clarity. Fourth, there needs to be simplification and unification of NGO fiscal treatment. And then we need the consolidation of a model and not constant and complex change. Regulations and requirements also need to be tailored according to the size of an organisation (at the moment, we have to report in the same way as big business).

The international review team felt that these insights and related proposals made a great deal of sense and were consistent with practice in many other European countries. It also felt, however, that legislation had not always been obtuse and obstructive. We will discuss youth justice below but the legal reform package relating to minors in the criminal justice system (and the measures that have flowed from that) provides evidence of the potential of reform to produce radical and progressive policy in one particular area of youth policy. It might be of interest to try to discern why such progress has been made in that field (a

---

20. Until it received feedback from the ministry, the international review team had heard nothing officially about this. The ministry reported the establishment of an Agency for Civil Society which already has a board and will be recruiting staff during February 2010.

21. The two-year time-scale was reported to the international review team during its visits in September and November 2009; however, it would appear from more recent information from the ministry (see footnote above) that the process has been accelerated.

22. The tax system in Hungary allows taxpayers to dedicate 2% of their taxes to a named NGO or, if they do not do this, automatically allocates 1% of their taxes to a civic fund that distributes resources to NGOs through a tendering process. It is a commendable, though far from ideal system. Though it appears to produce a strong resource base for NGOs, its distribution system is highly bureaucratic.

coherent, consistent and undivided lobby might be one explanation) while elsewhere legislation has more often been considered more of a hindrance than a help.

> **Recommendation 15**
>
> *The international review team is not persuaded that if something is enshrined in law in Albania, it happens. Law can be as obstructing as it can be enabling. There appears to be something of an obsession with legislative process: better and fewer laws might be a simple recommendation.*

## Delivery mechanisms

"It is a moment for civil society in Albania for the implementation of ideas." (youth NGO respondent)

There are reputedly some 6 000 NGOs in Albania. They may be registered as such, but many are inactive. In 2003, there were some 150 active youth organisations; today, there are no more than 40. It is in fact very difficult to establish the legitimacy and credibility of civil society organisations, as one respondent suggested:

Some are just fake, just registered and in receipt of funds because of their connections, without ever delivering or implementing their proposals and ideas. Even then, sometimes their funding is repeated.

The European Youth Forum (2007) reported that there were only 90-150 youth NGOs, "out of which three or four are active at national level". It noted that "many of the youth NGOs are not registered so it is difficult to fully detect their real number". Youth NGOs, as previous Council of Europe international reviews of national youth policies have confirmed, are an essential part of the jigsaw for the effective delivery of youth policy. Other pieces of that jigsaw are clearly the state, through regional and municipal structures and also more generic NGOs that may have some focus on young people and youth issues.

In Albania it would appear that the "vertical" links between the central government and regional and local administrations are still relatively underdeveloped (the youth centre proposals mentioned above may address this to some extent) and that more generic NGOs, with perhaps the exception of those concerned with disability and minorities, have limited focus on youth. Therefore, rather as in Lithuania during the 1990s (see Jasiukaityté and Reiter 2002; Breen et al. 2003), the role of youth NGOs may be pivotal to the delivery of services, projects and programmes.

The National Youth Strategy, formulated in 2006, was alert to the challenges facing youth NGOs and has a dedicated section (in Chapter II) on strengthening their capacities: "One of the most pressing needs of the youth sector is the strengthening of organizational and managerial capacities of youth organizations" (p. 13). The National Youth Strategy identifies three central problems: the transience of leadership and the resultant loss of knowledge transfer; weak channels of communication among actors in the youth field (for discussion of how such things can be improved, see Milmeister and Williamson 2006); and poor public relations resulting in a failure to optimise sources of financial and other support. The vision in the National Youth Strategy is to develop training in youth leadership, improve "fair practices" for monitoring the performance of youth organisations and encourage better communication and collaboration. The practical outcomes of this vision should be enhanced planning and co-ordination capacities among youth NGOs.

A somewhat different critical analysis of the current situation of youth NGOs was offered by the youth NGOs themselves:

> The biggest obstacle for us is resources and winning the support of donors, especially the US donors that have been very significant in the past 10-15 years. In recent years, there has been no capacity-building strategy for the youth sector. All attention is now directed towards European Union funds, and these are very hard to access (application, procedures and accountability). We need the involvement of public institutions, but they lack experience and sometimes commitment (both time and financial contributions). So the result is that Albania is likely to get just one or two projects. And then there can be the lack of transparency in these procedures. Civil society organisations are not informed at all, at least not in time to be able to respond properly to opportunities. This is a criticism of both the European Union and the Albanian government[23] and representatives of the European Union in this country. Everything needs to be more inclusive and we must ensure participation from the whole sector and from the whole country, those who currently don't really have a voice.

Nevertheless, many youth organisations agree with the analysis projected within the National Youth Strategy. Some, such as Partners Albania (see leaflet on Youth lidership [sic]) and Kriik, are actively involved in delivering leadership programmes, the latter with training, seminars and summer schools (including a summer university in Vlora). The theme of its current training programme is democracy and the enlargement of Europe. Partners Albania has developed a five-day training programme that covers issues such as leadership and management, conflict and change management, effective communication, and negotiation. This NGO has been providing training since 2001. Around 200 young people have taken part in its youth leadership programme and it has always tried to encourage the involvement of young people within its wider training activities. Significantly, it has worked largely outside Tirana "because plenty is going on there".

---

23. The ministry maintained that "several steps" have already been taken to address such concerns, such as the provision of a letter of reference for European funding applications by youth NGOs, and information-sharing on the ministry's website.

The range of training activities carried out by youth NGOs is impressive in its content (we know rather less about its coverage). Beyond those issues mentioned above, there has been attention given to:

- organisational skills;
- proposal writing;
- project management;
- participatory processes;
- taxation;
- legislation;
- gender.

More operational activity has included the provision of internships for young people to gain experience, a photography project on how those who study abroad might promote Albania as a place for tourism and the revival of traditional sports. On a more social level, there have been projects dedicated to supporting Roma children, training young people in doing "social" work such as encouraging non-smoking amongst high school students (through interventions made by medical students at the university), and action on the streets around issues such as domestic abuse.

Another respondent from a youth NGO testified to the "low status" of youth NGOs, a lack of communication between them and, consequently, considerable duplication of effort and focus. To address this, a network of youth NGOs was established with the intention of "bringing people together to co-operate better in the use of infrastructure (building space), skills and projects". It was claimed that the network has supported contact-making seminars, which have led to "some real concrete projects". In particular, it had broadened experience of international work. This led to a discussion, once more, of the obstacles within the Albanian context; it was much easier, it was argued, to work with the European framework. One commentator did not beat about the bush:

> Trying to work with the Albanian authorities is bureaucratic, sluggish ... sometimes they steal the ideas and the money is always delayed. This is a problem for most, if not all, NGOs. The public sector sometimes seems to assume that the NGO sector is rich, with all their money coming from international donors. There is a complete lack of acknowledgement that many of us are working voluntarily for much of the time.

This critique extended to the absence of any real support for the National Youth Council and its eventual demise. The National Youth Council had functioned from 1999 to 2004/5, but its last three years were bereft of projects (and it therefore had no resources) and it had depended completely on volunteers. It had become unsustainable and had collapsed. The prevailing view of many youth NGOs was that, though the National Youth Council had had "a lot of energy and committed people, it had no money and no support from the government". To some, the collapse of the National Youth Council symbolised the government's lack of interest in, or recognition of, the contribution made by the youth NGO sector to youth policy and its implementation.

Not that there is always complete separation and antagonism between the youth NGO sector and the public sector. Indeed, given that the ministry hosted the meetings between the international review team and the youth NGOs and given that the youth NGO sector made a significant contribution to the National Youth Strategy (the process was actually facilitated by Partners Albania), the gulf may be less pronounced than some of the hard-hitting remarks made by youth NGOs might suggest. An alternative interpretation would be that those remarks were generally directed beyond the Youth Ministry, whose staff are clearly equally committed to the same ends. And at a more local level, the youth centre in Fier had forged strong links with youth NGOs in order to extend support and endeavour to strengthen civil society in the area:

> Youth are critical to sustaining democratic development in Albania. We have a strategy to make contact with youth organisations and to engage them in our work. We also work with students at high school and universities. The process for building up civil society has been slowed considerably in recent years, so we are now working much more closely with civil society partners. The youth sector is dynamic and constantly changing, and it needs frequent renewal. Some youth organisations request assistance to build their capacity. They want to know how to do participatory processes and then welcome young people on board in that way.

In our discussions with various people about the delivery of services to young people, a constant target of criticism, indeed condemnation, was the establishment and subsequent behaviour of the NGO Mjaft ('Enough'). This was often described as an (allegedly spurious) NGO but perceived by the international review team to have been, at least initially, a rational conduit for the distribution of international (and national) donor funds to the youth sector. The story of Mjaft appears to be immensely complex, entangled with the evolving politics of Albania, and easily susceptible to widespread interpretations peppered with political innuendo. The international review team enters into this territory with considerable caution. As we understand it, Mjaft was formed at the instigation of the SOROS Foundation in 2003 and brought together all major donors as members of its board, "not just in Albania but from surrounding countries". Resources were then channelled through Mjaft which, to its critics, operated an "incestuous" and "nepotistic" regime. More charitable interpretations were expressed by two respondents who commented that:

> Originally Mjaft was a mechanism for civil society to connect with the political structures. I don't know any more what the relation is between Mjaft and political leaders, but that was the case and it was not a good thing.

> Mjaft started as a youth organisation but then took on some social roles and then moved into the political sphere. The NGO sector was not very strong. Mjaft had a lot of money from international donors. But now their leaders have moved on into politics. They are still linked to the NGOs but instead of leading them they are controlling them. So the situation has become very bad.

Outspoken youth NGOs claimed that Mjaft was riddled with corruption, served its own interests and often pretended to have undertaken "completely mythical work". In other words, the monopoly over resources secured through the creation of Mjaft had seriously undermined the capacity of the NGO sector to deliver to the youth field. Mjaft and the resources it had attracted had "created a funding desert for other youth NGOs in Albania".

Whatever the "truth" about the formation, development and activities of Mjaft (which appears to be a murky cocktail of many forces; Mjaft subsequently transmuted into a political party, G99, but it attracted only 20 000[24] of the 1.7 million votes cast), it is now history and there are now new approaches to the distribution of funds. The proposed National Youth Centre will agree a memorandum of understanding with youth NGOs and ensure greater transparency in the allocation of ministry (and other) funds. The legacy of Mjaft for the youth NGO sector is, quite clearly and very regrettably, a sustaining suspicion around the funding mechanisms for the sector.

---

**Recommendation 16**

*The international review team believes that an independent grant-giving structure for the youth NGO sector is urgently needed, to advise on the distribution of governmental resources and to act as a sounding board for other potential donors. There are models of this kind from other countries. In Albania, given the prevailing perspectives on recent history, it is likely to be the only way of restoring trust and confidence in funding mechanisms.*

---

"Promises, promises ... but nothing happens ..." (youth NGO respondent)

As many of those who spoke to the international review team suggested, it is relatively easy to envision what could and should be done for young people in Albania. Notwithstanding the inevitable resource challenges, young people are essentially local and therefore "local practice needs cementing". The international review team observed and learned about a diversity of interesting and innovative practice around youth policy but constantly wondered whether or not these are isolated, temporary and atypical projects, rather than part of some more structural and structured approach. Indeed, through listening and learning about such practice, the international review team felt there were some key issues that demand far more substantial attention:

- sustainability into the medium term;
- regional and local strategies (bottom up and top down);
- a "local" base: youth centres;
- governmental lead;
- cross-sectoral approaches;
- communication and knowledge transfer.

---

24. The ministry corrected this figure that was mentioned in discussions, pointing that the Election Central Commission had registered just under 12 500 votes for this party.

**Government-identified issues**

## Sustainability into the medium term

With few exceptions, delivery appears to be contingent on the capacity of youth NGOs (or sometimes municipal youth centres) to find external funds for dedicated projects. Quite how the ideas for such projects are generated is unclear. Sometimes the genesis for them is commendable, often through consultation with young people (see below), but sometimes they can be "donor-driven" which may not in itself be a bad thing but can tend towards distorting the nature of provision. Young people often do not really care who provides services and experiences, so long as they can access them. What is needed is a basic "youth offer", covering some core "entitlements", grounded in some core "principles" and subject to some established "methods". The detail is not to be prescribed here, but an illustration would be careers advice, health care, leisure-time association and holiday experiences, based around principles of participation and education (learning), and provided through individual support, group work and activity-based programmes. One reputable NGO would be charged with ensuring that such an offer reaches an agreed proportion of the youth population, through both direct and indirect delivery. This would be contracted on a renewable time-frame – subject to review – of perhaps three years. Such arrangements would produce a level of stability and certainty that has hitherto not existed in the youth field in Albania. The basic offer could, of course, be "topped up" with more dedicated projects financed through successful applications to donors, but the lead youth NGO would have a more secure anchor for development.

## Regional and local strategies

National legislation, visions, strategies and plans have to incorporate thinking about decentralisation. Otherwise, things go nowhere or any action simply gets "stuck" in the centre. Beyond the youth field, the international review team was concerned that Albania did not appear to have a regional strategy (see above) but, for national youth policy to establish "coverage" of the nation in question, there have to be vertical arrangements for delivery. This is not simply a "top-down" challenge; there is also an imperative for a "bottom-up" momentum, where local action can meet national strategy. This is a further reason for consolidating and developing current practice rather than seeking to effect yet more change. Investing in credible local youth NGOs (or national youth NGOs working at the local level) in order to develop and diversify youth practice is the mechanism for building from the ground, rather than just trying to respond to instruction from the top. In Fier – an industrial town, though many of its factories are now closed – the youth centre has been enabling young people to contribute prominent youth issues to the local municipal plans. Relevant employment, particularly for university graduates who come back (there is only one private university in Fier, so many young people have to study elsewhere), is a pressing issue. It has been addressed through a labour fair in 2008, the production of a guide to the types of professional (such as engineers) who are most needed in the town, and the provision of a course for young people at age 18 in all high schools – Orientation for Life – that focuses on careers and employment. These are not original ideas, but they are probably needed in similar contexts throughout Albania, and it is not clear that comparable provision is made elsewhere.

## A local base: youth centres

The youth centre in Fier is a modest setting – little more than an office and a meeting room – but it serves as the hub for a range of youth activities (of which we will learn more below in the discussion of youth participation). In contrast, in Durrës, the Youth Associations' council no longer has its "youth centre" (which had supported youth activity and reached vulnerable young people) because the high school in which it was located needed the space back. As a result, young people in Durrës felt that the momentum of their commitment and activities had slowed down. A physical base, even in a technological age (and Albania is less advanced technologically than many other European countries), is a critical asset for association, debate and development. It brings young people together to share ideas, think up projects and engage in activities. It can provide the first port of call for young people in need of social care, careers advice, jobs counselling, or drugs information. This does not mean that a youth centre can necessarily directly provide such services but it can offer the signposts and the support to access the appropriate services elsewhere.

## Governmental lead

Governments and their policies invariably attract criticism and sometimes vitriolic condemnation. Albania is no exception and there is perhaps more reason for some of these attacks. Nevertheless, its government is the democratically elected political authority and it therefore has a mandate to shape the nature of its desired youth policy.

The international review team acknowledges the huge input into emergent "youth policy" in Albania from international NGOs and recognises its importance over the past two decades. Now, though, it is perhaps time for the government to take more robust ownership and leadership of its framework for youth policy and to build on the indigenous skills that have developed, in the youth NGO sector and beyond, over the past decade. Whatever the youth NGO sector may say about the bureaucratic challenges of engaging with the Albanian context and favouring finding support beyond Albania's borders, the Albanian authorities need to celebrate the fact that it now has an experiential body of knowledge that no longer needs to be subordinated to the dictate and priorities of the international NGO sector. That sector has, as we have said, contributed enormously to providing a platform for development in youth policy, but the National Youth Strategy, and the branches of youth policy that are growing from it, needs to represent the framework within which international (and other) donors, and youth NGOs should be expected to operate. This will require a commitment to slowly changing the balance of funding made available for the delivery of youth policy and, critically, if grounded support is to be given to this proposal, sharper evidence from the Youth Ministry of a clear path from policy to practice.

## Cross-sectoral approaches

All countries have a "youth policy" – by intent, default or neglect (Williamson 2002). The point about this statement is that young people exist somewhere, and wherever that is, they are affected by the intentional and unintentional circumstances around them. That is their "youth policy" context. Thus the environmental concerns of Bushat Commune are very much linked to, and drawn from, prospects for young people. Young people will stay if they have leisure and employment opportunities, but they will also be concerned that they and their future families can live in a safe and healthy climate.

Hence the importance of cross-sectoral, or "joined-up", approaches to youth policy. This was sometimes very evident already in Albania, at both national and local levels, notably in the connections that have been made between health and education, on sexual health, smoking and alcohol and drugs issues. On other matters, such as internationalism and Europe, at national level, there seemed to be a complete absence of communication between the relevant ministries. The point here is that, at all levels of governance and practice (Ministries of Health, Justice, and Education, for example; or police officers, social workers and psychologists), there need to be structured arrangements for contact, communication and potential collaboration across the key youth policy themes of education, vocational training and employment, health, housing and justice, and the cross-cutting questions of lifelong learning, social inclusion, active citizenship, and personal and community safety. The international review team could provide myriad examples of why such cross-sectoral approaches are so important, but it is probably more important for those in Albania to identify these issues in relation to the current context and lifestyles of its young people.

## Communication and knowledge transfer

In the youth NGO field, the international review team met with the same individuals on more than one occasion. There does appear to be a small caucus of highly committed (and experienced) people working in this field who are "present on every stage". Nothing should detract from what they have offered and continue to offer but, as the National Youth Strategy rightly notes, there is an issue of communication and knowledge transfer, particularly across the "generations" of activists in youth NGOs. The dissemination of good practice is considered, within the Council of Europe's framework of youth policy (Williamson 2002; 2008), to be one of the underpinning foundations for the evolution of effective youth policy (alongside youth research, and the training of professional practitioners in the youth field). Beyond word of mouth, and the training courses offered by some youth NGOs (see above), the international review team wondered how youth practice ideas, issues and methodologies were disseminated to a wider population of possible or aspiring youth practitioners.

The international review team was left in no doubt that there are deep concerns about the strength and sustainability of delivery mechanisms for youth policy in Albania. Governmental structures that penetrate to the local level are weak, and much depends on the vision and commitment of youth NGOs, which themselves struggle to establish a sustainable position for either the consolidation or development of work they may have pioneered, through projects supported by the international donor community.

Such weaknesses are broadly recognised, at the level of politics, within the administration and amongst youth NGOs themselves. There is, however, a new optimism from the ministry and a cautious optimism amongst the youth NGOs in relation to the proposed National Youth Centre. The international review team is also only cautiously optimistic, for the idea has been "on the table" for some years. Indeed, the European Youth Forum, following its study visit in May 2007, noted:

> The first task for the ministry is to establish an agency for youth that would increase the staff and budget for youth. The agency would support the youth work in the country, assist the project administration and act as the main interlocutor for youth issues from the side of the Albanian Government. The government has asked assistance from the UK Government and UNDP for the project of establishing the agency. (European Youth Forum 2007)

No-one is in fact very clear what the role and responsibilities of the "agency" (now "centre") will be. At one point it was suggested that it might take over the registration of youth NGOs from the courts[25] and have the authority to strengthen delivery structures at regional and local levels. But it does have enormous potential. If it is to take the lead in youth policy in Albania, strategically and operationally, it could co-ordinate at least the following: training, information and youth information, international work, youth participation and empowerment, relations between government and the NGO sector (and within the NGO sector), central administration and local government. This would constitute both an overarching and an underpinning role. It would demand cross-party support from the parliament, would need to be quasi-independent, and be accountable to the relevant youth minister. Like so much else in Albania, the idea holds promise, but has yet to be put into effect.

---

25. The ministry informed the international review team that the planned National Youth Centre would not be responsible for the registration of youth NGOs.

## Youth participation

The low level of youth participation in decision-making process is a matter of critical concern for the consolidation of democratic governance in the country, as well as the achievement of sustainable social and economic development. The disregard of youth perspectives implicates significant costs in both political and economic terms. (Ministry of Tourism, Culture, Youth and Sports 2006, p. 13)

"The lack of involvement by young people is a cultural problem. It comes from history, when we had a dictatorship and people were not allowed to have initiative and involvement. They were told what to do. So there is no tradition of activism. People advance their own interests, there is not an agenda for the wider good." (young person, member of a youth participatory structure)

"It is not just a question of generations, but also about changing the thinking, mentality and culture of other professionals, so that they are more open and more receptive to dialogue and debate with young people. The mentality is still evolving!" (youth NGO respondent)

"We now have the best ever representation of young people in the real parliament, but they don't really change anything for young people!" (youth participation advocate)

Since the rather damning "situation analysis" in the National Youth Strategy (above) and a resultant "vision" to promote "more active youth participation in all levels of decision-making" (p. 15), quite considerable progress in the area of youth participation appears to have been made. The National Youth Strategy itself has aspirations that there should be 20% guaranteed youth participation at all levels of governance in Albania.

As the international review team concluded its second visit to Albania, it learned that moves were afoot to re-establish (or relaunch) the Albanian National Youth Council. The press release announcing this is reproduced below. We include this because many of those active and committed representatives of youth NGOs whom we met during our two visits have been party to these developments. The international review team had been deeply concerned that the NGO sector, whatever its political, philosophical and sometimes professional differences, had, for some years, been unable to find common cause in advocating collectively for the sector. Once again, however, there does appear to be some hope for the (re-) establishment of a democratic youth participation structure at the national level.

*21 November 2009*
*PRESS RELEASE*
*For immediate release*

**Civil Society reaffirms the will for re-establishing Albanian Youth Council and has initiated a new period of Representing Civil Society in Albania**
Today organizations of Civil Society gathered in the XII Assembly invited by 15 youth organizations in the celebration of the 15 anniversary of the creation of Youth Council. During XII Assembly of AYC, civil society organizations expressed their will to support the initiative of re-establishing AYC as an independent national structure which will represent Albanian Youth.

**Institutional Re-establishment of Albanian Youth Council**
At the beginning of the XII Assembly the organizations checked in and the representation mandates were verified and then succeeded the voting process for the creation of AYC. The new Board of AYC was elected based on the one member-one vote principle. In the meeting room there were 22 youth organizations (1 observer) while there are 28 confirmed member organizations and 9 others other expected to confirm.
The members of the Assembly and the representatives who were present during the discussions agreed that AYC is very necessary to support the youth organizations for building networks and European Integration.

**The past experience during the years 1994-2007: A basis we should start from**
Many discussions were also based on the topic of the 15 year history and experience of AYC (evaluated for its unusual contribution during the years 1994-2007, and the vacuum created during the 2 last years as a result of being blocked concerning the activities due to financial reasons and artificial difficulties created by dishonest competition supported by certain circles for political reasons. We should learn from experience how to reorganize and rebuild the network of youth organizations in Albania especially now that Albania is making steps towards European Integration.
Albanian Youth Council has given a huge contribution in the creation of a new beginning of Albanian Youth Leadership and nowadays all youth forums of political parties are led by leaders who had managing roles in AYC during the year 2000. AYC has played a crucial role in re-inforcing and supporting civil society in Albania and for this reason it has been evaluated at a national and international level by "NGO Civil Society Award" given by USAID in 2000 as well as in 2005 by OSCE/ODIHR for its contribution with 1000 observers who volunteered 100% during the elections held at that time.
During the meeting the representatives estimated that AYC should be a "bridge" between organizations themselves and local as well as international Institutions regarding issues that directly concern young people. It was also stressed the necessity to implement together with the Department of Policies for Youth of the Ministry of Culture the National Strategy for Youth 2007-2013 by also suggesting a concrete Action Plan within this Strategy as well as National Action Plan 2007-2013. What's more, the representatives of Civil Society highlighted the fact that AYC has a key role in capacity building of youth organisations offering services such as legal consulting, training courses, proper infrastructure and logistics. Member organizations of AYC and the rest of the representatives expressed the need for the creation of Local Youth Centers and asked from the AYC to closely co-operate with local and central powers in order to offer information on the European Union and the Integration process. In addition, Youth Parliaments will be also included very soon, created by AYC in 2000 with the support of UNICEF.

Government-identified issues

**The XII Assembly of AYC unanimously decided:**

1. Institutional and public Re-establishment of AYC as a supportive organisation NYC (National Youth Council) by encouraging all Albanian youth organisations as "Observer Members" to become members of the biggest and oldest organisation in Albania which now will play an active role in civil society in order to create the proper and deserved space.

2. Since Albania has already initiated the procedures towards European Integration, and fulfills the standards and criteria required for the Visa Liberalisation Process, AYC should play an active role in integrating Albanian organisations into European structures and contribute with expertise, participation and spreading information with regard to the agenda of the European Integration of Albania.

3. The reinforcement of the role of youth organisations focusing on the issues of employment of young people, vocational training for a healthy society, and enhancing the quality of education.

4. Raising awareness and providing information for the young people regarding the decision-making process and elections in Albania.

5. Reinforcement of youth leadership at a local and central level, promoting gender balance through training, qualification and promotion of Youth Leadership, by taking as an example the experience of AYC itself since 1994 – something which has really contributed to this field and has given young people capabilities and valuable skills for their careers.

6. AYC will start the procedures towards the reinforcement of a special legal and economic status for young people by co-operating with the Ministry of Education and Science and the Department of Policies for Youth of the Ministry of Culture, including the Students' Card and European Card for Young People EURO‹26, according to European Standards, based also on the interrupted experience of AYC in 2007 due to financial difficulties and great pressure created during the years 2003-2007 by certain circles.

In order to start a fast stabilization of the Albanian Youth Council, the Assembly decided that within a short period to start working on the "Days of Youth" which will take place on 28 November - 8 December 2009, and it was also created an Organizative Committee which will co-ordinate the work with the Department of Policies for Youth, at the Ministry of Culture, within the framework of national activities of "Days of Youth". In addition, the Assembly decided on re-establishing the contacts with homologous International Institutions AYC aspires to be member of.

The confirmed participating organizations in the Albanian Youth Council until 21 November 2009:

1. European Law Student Association – ELSA (International NGO) Albania

2. Student in Free Enterprise – SIFE * (International NGO) Albania

3. Albanian Student Abroad Network – AS@N *

4. Youth Group of SOS Village * (International NGO) Albania

5. Albania Youth Press – part of European Youth Press (International NGO)

6. European Youth Parliament Albania – (International NGO) Dega Shqipëri

7. Young European Federalists – Albania – JEF – Albania (International NGO)

8. Youth Group of the Centre on Population and Development (International NGO)

9. Young European Liberals – Albania

10. Youth Group for Human Rights A+ (Action Plus)

11. Youth Centre – Vlora

12. Albanian Centre for Integration of Young People

13. Albanian Environmentalist Students Club – KSASH

14. Centre of Education and Civic Participation

15. Students for Students – S4S

16. Youth Associations Council – Durrës

17. Youth Club of Office of Consumer Protection

18. "Art Contact" Centre

19. First Step Association

20. Youth Shaker

21. Association 16+

22. Association for Integration and Development

23. Associate for Sportive Culture and Recreation "PRO-ALBANIA"

24. ZMIMSC Foundation – Gjirokastër*

25. Social Club – Korçë*

26. National Students Council (Observer Member)

27. Students Council of University of Tirana (Observer Member)*

The organisations with the sign (*) were not present at the Assembly and for technical reasons they confirmed their membership at the Albanian Youth Council.

**On behalf of the Secretariat Commission of Albanian Youth Council**
Respectfully,
**Vladimir Thano**
**President of JEF Albania**
**Young European Federalists Albania**
info@jefalbania.org
Tel: +355692500850

Despite the problems that have dogged the National Youth Council in recent years (according to the European Youth Forum 2007, "political clashes and disagreements among the members and the leadership") youth participation in other parts of the youth field and at more local levels is arguably the "jewel in the crown" of Albanian youth policy. The international review team met with young people in a number of places, some formal members of "youth parliaments", others simply interested in talking to us, and others (usually slightly older) interested in making some commitment to their younger peers. We were usually deeply impressed.

The momentum for the promotion of child and youth participation originated with Save the Children in Albania. Although its initiatives are based firmly within the United Nations Convention on Children's Rights (UNCRC) a spectrum of approaches to participation have now been established by a range of organisations and projects. Yet, despite the considerable progress that has been made, it was conceded that "there are still a lot of obstacles from the community about child participation, because obviously this was not part of the former culture". Concerns were also expressed that various initiatives on child and youth participation had created "happy islands, rather than meaningful participation" on account of the self-selection of more privileged young people. To some extent, however, this issue had been addressed in relation to the "children's governments" (see below) – once there was awareness of the "problem", through learning about parental occupations – which "made us start to think how to do things differently". More inclusive criteria were established and more concerted efforts were made to reach "the more marginalised".

### Children's governments

The children's governments (sometimes referred to, or translated as, student governments) are a requirement enshrined in Albanian law, for every school in the pre-university system. Every class elects their representative (or senator) and then they elect the president of the school. There is a booklet setting out the procedures that have to be followed. The president of the children's government is a member of the board of the school, though – significantly – we were told that "they may not have a vote".

The objective is to "reinforce and empower student participation in school governance", though it was noted that too often the children's governments were less about strengthening the exercise of children's rights in schools and more "about organising recreational activities rather than more central issues". Indeed, it was said that children were only permitted to address "second-hand" issues, not central aspects of schooling, such as curriculum or discipline. To combat this trend, Save the Children was endeavouring to build advisory groups of children across the seven regions of central and southern Albania in relation to education planning structures. The goal will be to improve children's contribution to decision making through membership of school boards, preparing school development plans, determining optional curricula for schools and informing school regulations.

Child participation is, of course, a cross-cutting issue and, in three regions (Elbasan, Durrës and Peshkopi) there are groups of children operating at town level rather than just school level and contributing to broader forms of governance. In Elbasan, a group of children have produced a child-friendly version of the UNCRC. The group became national "experts" in children's rights, called itself Voice 16+ and expanded to other cities: hence the formation of groups in Durrës and Peshkopi. One of the benefits of these developments was forging links with young people who were no longer at school and other more marginalised groups. There are concerns about the sustainability of such initiatives, though these three groups are now replacing themselves "as the oldest members move on". But the existence of such groups remains contingent on the goodwill of adults, notably the mayor. Save the Children is keen to ensure a stronger Memorandum of Understanding with local authorities "so that children's participation is embedded in their practice".

In Bushat, the small group of young people who came, along with many others, to a meeting with the international review team, were direct about their issues and their demands. "I come here to raise the voice of young people from my high school", said one assertively. They were part of the children's government[26] whose role was described as "bringing the problems that students have to the student leader and then he *[sic]* passes it to the school board and the director". Generally they organised activities, visits and competitions. They felt that attention was given to issues directly related to the school, particularly regarding relationships with students, "but then there are other things, wider things, that don't get solved". These appeared to be forms of provision which had huge financial implications: mainly sports and leisure facilities.

At the national level, the Inter-Ministerial Committee on Children, responsible for producing the national strategy on children, has held an annual conference looking at developments and achievements. Government and NGOs have always been involved but, since 2007, children have also been involved. The international review team applauds all of these developments. It is important to remember that the UNCRC has just celebrated its 20th anniversary and there remains much to be done, even in those countries that theoretically embraced it right from the start. Regrettably, the Albanian Children's Alliance's "alternative report" to the UN is not (yet) available in English but, whatever criticisms it may have made, the international review team hopes that it also celebrated the achievements that have been made over a relatively short space of time.

---

26. Like the young people from the Youth Parliament in Durrës, these young people had professional aspirations (three to be lawyers, three to be nurses and one to be a teacher). All but one of their mothers, however, did not have paid work and were described as "housewives" or "at home". Two fathers were professionals (a teacher and an army officer), one owned a bar, one had emigrated to Greece, one was a taxi driver, one worked in a car wash and the other was a farmer.

### Youth parliaments

Youth parliaments are different from children's governments in that they address issues beyond school boundaries and activities beyond the school. There are, nonetheless, some overlapping areas of focus, such as school security and the content of school books, but the roles and purpose of the two structures are different. Youth parliaments, composed of young people aged 11-14 years and 15-19 years, are, for legal reasons, usually managed and facilitated by local NGOs. Their evolution has been supported by UNICEF, with the express intention of "young people making public the issues that affect their futures". UNICEF has sought to find local mechanisms for productive relationships between youth parliaments and local authorities. In Durrës, for example, there is a local youth plan within which there is an intention to spend 2% of the local budget on youth activities.

Examples of some of the significant, "profile" achievements of the youth parliament network include the law prohibiting the sale of alcohol to under 18s. This was initiated by the youth parliament in one particular district. The district council established its own prohibitions that eventually turned into national law. Another example was around the protection of the environment, a debate that is continuing.

Youth parliaments are primarily focused on issues within the boundaries of their regions, but from time to time there are parliamentary days when they come together in Tirana for information, training and the exchange of experiences and the topics they have been addressing (such as unemployment, substance use, or trafficking). There is, on these occasions, a day in the national parliament, with their order of business and the presentation of their priority issues and related calls for action. One example of this was a campaign against corruption when a 14-year-old girl said to the speaker of the parliament that she wanted to grow up in a society where the role models/heroes were not just those who had made a fortune overnight.

As with the children's governments, there are significant challenges in engaging with more disadvantaged and excluded young people. The international review team was interested in how, if one in five young people stop their formal schooling around the age of 14 or 15, young people from this group might be involved. The response was that there are efforts to involve both ethnic and language minorities and those who are already out of school, largely through outreach methods. There may be better mechanisms, "but so far this is the way the issue has been addressed". The extent to which such groups had become involved in youth parliaments was mixed: "it is not very exciting to sit around and debate many issues, but some issues can be energising and exciting, particularly when you can give examples of impact and success". Apparently, the use of different recycling waste bins was originally an idea of the youth parliament in Tirana.

The international review team met with the youth parliament of Durrës (Parlamenti Rinor Durrës) which was now in its seventh year of existence. We were told what it did:

> We are a sort of network. Since our establishment, there have been representatives of local institutions and local government involved in our work. We have to have

permission from local high schools. But our central task is capacity building for our members – to promote the voice of young people both inside and outside schools. We cover a lot of youth issues: drug abuse, delinquency, smoking, decision making, voting for first-time voters, women candidates for elections, awareness activities, protests, environment issues (this is one of the most polluted areas in Albania and the Balkans), entertainment activities, wanting to re-open a youth centre that was closed in 2002. We will see if the MPs of Durrës keep their promises to us!

The international review team was also interested in its level of autonomy and independence and what kinds of democratic procedures shaped its "constitution". The following is a synthesis of their responses:

We are a project of UNICEF and we are not independent. We are part of an umbrella structure, which in Durrës is the Council of Youth Associations. But we do have high credibility with the work we do. We are related to the general high schools where there are the separate governments of students (the children's governments), and they elect people to be members of the youth parliament. There are also volunteers who give assistance but who do not have a vote. Two vice-presidents and a president are elected from the membership. Elections are carried out every year. We prepare a programme of activities and then tell people what we have done. And the representatives from schools can always take back information to their schools. They have been elected through election campaigns in schools, open campaigns with real voting processes, through collaboration with the children's governments of the schools. Three deputies are elected from each school, but not from the final year (though those can come as ordinary members). There is one candidate put forward from each class, so there are between five and seven candidates usually in each school. There is a secret ballot, then an open count. Candidates campaign to get elected, sometimes controversially through things like posters on the school walls. All schools are involved, including the three vocational schools in Durrës, though there are problems engaging the private schools and some of them do not take part. We have not conducted elections there, but have had volunteer members. The background of the deputies is not relevant,[27] it is simply about their capacity and competence – contributing something. There used to be more girls than boys, now there are more boys than girls! We are careful to respect some gender balance; vice-presidents are always one girl and one boy.

The Durrës Youth Parliament has 25 deputies and meets once a week after school lessons finish, at around 2 p.m. Attendance is sometimes an issue: deputies from more outlying areas do not come so often because of the travel costs (about € 1, which is expensive). The youth parliament has a co-ordinator whose role is to "take care" of the planning and the monitoring of how its work takes shape,

---

27. We asked the members of the Youth Parliament about their parents' occupations and it was a social mix, although they leaned towards the professions. Parents were teachers, an engineer, a sailor, a ship's officer, a tailor, a construction worker and a housewife. The young people themselves had high professional aspirations: lawyer, dentist, surgeon and "something in the social field".

"but the parliament decides what is wanted or needs to be done". Currently, the youth parliament is based in the Palace of Culture but one of its campaigns is for some separate premises. It conducts campaigns on what it considers to be significant local issues affecting young people (the current flagship campaign relates to the anticipated environmental damage that would arise if planned building work proceeds in Porto Romano) and it runs projects. There remains, apparently, considerable dependency on UNICEF "which is the only donor to youth parliaments". Other donors are reluctant to provide support when these structures are so closely associated with UNICEF.

We asked the youth parliament members whether their parents were supportive of this work, or if they were concerned about so much energy and time being "diverted" from their studies and school work:

> There is a more comprehensive view about empowerment and involvement these days and generally our parents have understood this very well. It is not just about study any more. We have also shown that our involvement in the Youth Parliament has not impeded our studies or success in high school. We need this organisation to help other young people to take part more in activities and in society more generally – responsibility and open mindedness, like in other countries. It is not so hard to persuade our friends, but sometimes it can be quite difficult for them to persuade their parents. I think it is harder with those from the less urban areas.

As we have noted above, there are youth parliaments in all 12 regions, and the Durrës Youth Parliament co-operates with their counterparts elsewhere. However, there is no national youth parliament providing the apex to the structure at a national level. Mention was made of the National Youth Council – in the past tense! Though youth parliaments can promote issues related to politics (such as the right to vote), they are not permitted to campaign for political parties. Debates on the practical matters that concern them are organised strictly through the institutions of civil society (youth NGOs, and the Council of Youth Associations).

The international review team did not meet any young people from the youth parliament in Fier, but heard from the youth centre workers about the evolution of its work (see also below). The Fier Youth Parliament had been established in 2004, with the support of UNICEF. The youth centre had "opened" two years later, "although there was no real building, but things had progressed and we had used the offices of others for training". Eventually the youth centre had acquired a building and developed a number of projects. There are now three professionals attached to the work of the youth centre. The Youth Parliament meets weekly and carries out most of its activities on weekends, in collaboration with other structures and other NGOs. In 2009, it held its third week-long summer school, which looked at the rights of young people, using the Council of Europe's human rights manual, *Compass*. Eighteen young people took part. The Youth Parliament is now at the heart of a wider range of participatory practices and projects supported through the youth centre in Fier (see below).

The Youth Parliament of Tirana provided the international review team with a written precis of its core objectives and the work carried out in 2008 and planned in 2009:

> Youth Participation in the decision-making process is our main objective. More than 40 000 students, aged between 14 and 19 years, live and study in Tirana, to which we have give the space to elect and to be elected in Youth Parliament, and represent the youth voice at local decision making.

In 2008, it was involved in citizens' commissions (on issues such as sports, arts and culture, environment, health, violence and crime, education, enterprise and information technology), budgetary discussions, youth groups of the "mini-municipalities" of Tirana (through Memoranda of Understanding), local action plans – and it also contributed to various national strategies and plans. During 2009, it hoped to raise the participation levels of young women and first-time voters for the Youth Parliament, sign more Memoranda of Understanding with other "mini-municipalities" of Tirana (thus increasing youth participation in local government), inject youth issues into the party political campaigns for the election (June 2009), educate young people about the right to vote, broaden societal understanding of gender balance and youth participation, give more marginalised young people more voice (by providing 10 places on the Youth Parliament for Roma young people), and building capacity through training and workshops. For a relatively small group of young people, making these commitments during their "spare" time, this is an ambitious and demanding work programme. The international review team was suitably impressed.

During one meeting with youth NGOs, the international review team was introduced to a youth NGO called the European Youth Parliament. This is quite distinct from those developments described above. The idea of the "European Youth Parliament" was established in France some 22 years ago. Its roots in Albania were planted just three years ago but it "only really got going a year ago", receiving support from European Youth Parliaments elsewhere, especially those in Italy and France:

> So far we have organised two round table debates modelled on the proceedings of the European Parliament, producing resolutions and decisions. This has involved young people who have had more than 20 experiences outside Albania and we are now ready to organise our own international event. We are getting to know more about the European issues, the working of the European Union and the challenges within the European Union although we are not European Union citizens. It has been hard to get the support of institutions inside Albania but we are getting ready to expand what we are doing. So far there is only a Tirana branch but we want to broaden our geographical base and sustain the national forums. We have sent members to Sweden, France and Finland: recruiting and training them to be more active in EYP and to be more active citizens more generally. Our spirit has been one of bringing innovation. For 20 years in Albania we have been hoping and waiting for changes and we know that small changes contribute to bigger changes. We hope we operate in a professional way. Our target group is 16- to 19-year-olds but there is also space for students and older young people.

The European Youth Parliament held its first international event, in Durrës, at the end of November 2009 – a significant achievement for one of the many forms of youth participation which have grown in Albania in recent years.

## Student councils

The international review team understands that, within the higher education system, there are student councils that contribute to the governance and infrastructure of universities. It did not, however, receive a great deal of information on this form of participation. There is, of course, a long tradition on this front in many other parts of Europe, though clearly not in Albania, as our only respondent to speak about this testified:

> I was active with friends when I was at high school and then at university I saw there was nothing. I was concerned about the passivity of students so, with some friends, talked about being more active. We established a bigger group, had elections and now have a participative place in the faculty. In Albania there are efforts by young people to have a greater presence and be a bigger force, something to be listened to, but it needs more time; it will take more time. Our strategy has two parts: empowerment (you can be a force) and making a social life (providing something to do). Many young people are not really active and "do not live in the community", but when they get the chance, they like it and want to do it more. We need to build the reputation of the value of engaging with youth parliaments: in terms of future job prospects and so on. The big dilemma always: those who stand for elections but don't know why; those who would be good people to stand, but who are not likely to do so!! There are a lot of good people who could make a difference. Young people who have done training in other countries often bring good ideas back here and want to implement them with others. But there is still a problem of lack of collaboration with the presidents of other university student councils.

The international review team was not aware that students' councils were so recent. But clearly they are a further rung on a ladder for the participation of young people – within school, in their local communities and then in higher education. Alongside the 25 youth NGOs invited to be members, the National Students' Council and the Student Council of Tirana University have been affiliated to the new National Youth Council "because of their size and the contribution they can make".

## Youth work initiatives

The Youth Parliament in Fier seems to have been the catalyst and foundation for the very active engagement of young people in planning issues within the municipality. The youth centre has established a pilot project entitled Youth Agent for Change. In 2008, the youth centre had drafted an action plan for youth at the local level and, with international donor support effort has been made to put this plan into practice through the cultivation of co-operation and discussion with the local authorities "for the first time in years". Workshops, involving young people and personnel from relevant municipal directorates and government departments, were organised on different themes within the strategy. Though the elections of 2009 slowed down the process, the youth centre is now waiting for municipal approval of the action plan for 2010. The impressive range of youth "engagement" in Fier is worth reporting just as the international review team learned about it:

> In addition to activities we have organised international days and built programmes of activities based on the needs of young people. The Youth Parliament is a central tool for this since, after the parliament is elected through a process involving every school (there are 12 high schools in town), and therefore there are 36 representatives from these schools. Young people are very committed and energetic and then are also trained by us; for example, the poster that illustrates the effort of our group for three main issues prior to the elections of 28th June. Gjanican – pollution of the river. Punësimi – youth unemployment. Stadiumi – stadium. Young people lobbied politicians so these things would be in their electoral manifesto and programme. Many young people (120) assisted with the work of the election, monitoring and serving the process. Another campaign that we are still continuing is the promotion of voluntary activities with special emphasis on environmental issues, which is very important in Albania but particularly important in our time. We have also been pressing for the introduction of a new curriculum in the schools. Our centre has been leading in promoting awareness of these things in schools. Young people are involved in voluntary work every weekend. Another of our main activities and one which has been important from the very beginning is the summer school on leadership and decision making. We focus on the rights of young people (using Compass) and do not only lectures there but also enable young people to participate in their own activities decided on by them. Another activity that has been running for four years has been participation in budgeting: young people promote such processes carried out within the municipality and give their opinions on these issues. Since 2005, young people have been part of the commission for the planning and implementation of the budget of the municipality. So if in previous years we just assisted in the process, now we are more centrally part of the process. There has also been a youth commission created for the municipality. Youth groups have always been active and close to the municipality but they have never before been so close to involvement in decision making. This will be the focus in 2011, especially because local elections will be held at that time. Beyond the promotion of female participation there will also be an emphasis on youth participation. So that is the general description of what we do.

Young people had been contributing their views on the municipal budgeting process for four years but, in 2009, played a much more active part in planning local public expenditure. In particular, they had been monitoring provision in each of the four areas of the town and identified one project that they would like to see supported from the municipal budget in each of these areas. The outcome of this input is currently awaited.

Though many of these developments are to be applauded, the international review team wondered how much young people were simply accepting of the initial strategy framework established by the municipality, or whether there was room for criticism and even confrontation. The international review team was assured that the "youth work" in Fier is firmly based on what young people perceive to be their needs and concerns, which are then communicated to the municipality, whether or not the municipality considers them to be important.

### Non-organised youth

One group of young people who had no connection with formal structures but nevertheless were willing to share their views with the international review team was the group of 15 young people we met at the Roma community centre in Shkodra. Unlike the formal groups, they did not talk about wider "political" issues (such as environment, or Europe) but about their more immediate needs: work and income, education and training, health and welfare. None of the parents of these young people, aged between 13 and 18, had a job; they themselves did not always attend school and seized opportunities to work (for example, unloading the cargo of trucks). The young people talked of improving their knowledge and finding futures in dance and music, computers and languages. But they, alongside their contemporaries, still went begging in the street and, when asked about getting involved in more formal structures supporting the "voice of young people", simply said that had neither the time nor the information about such possibilities.

It was a rather more optimistic picture at the Roma community centre in Tirana, where a very educated group of young Roma people was contributing to development and activities. They rejected the suggestion that they were some kind of elite, maintaining that decisions about programme development at the centre were taken on a "round table" basis, involving "all sides, and all levels of education". They said that some of their programme was holding discussions in schools and universities, where they could "show both Roma culture and traditions, and how we have integrated through education and involvement". This small group had already produced the first edition of a magazine concerned with pride in being Roma and recounting some Roma cultural history. They were also planning to write some material about living within (or between?) two cultures. They described themselves as a group "that wants to create change" and, with the blend of their commitment and their rather unique personal profiles, appear to be doing so.

Even at the 'special needs school' (community social centre) in Kombinat, the director said that young people had some opportunity to contribute to the framing of their learning needs and plans, whereas in the past this was simply determined entirely by the professional staff.

Without descending into some of the more theoretical debates about the meaning and "authenticity" of youth participation (even though this does exercise many minds), one can be complimentary to the Albanian context for having sought to grow a range of prospective participatory structures and possibilities for young people, albeit with the catalytic support of dedicated international NGOs (notably Save the Children and UNICEF). There are, of course, questions that need to be asked, but these should not detract from the significant and impressive progress that has been made on this front in a relatively short space of time. There are, nevertheless, questions that merit reflection and debate.

First there is the question of coverage. How many young people avail themselves of these opportunities and what kinds of young people take part? More to the point, are there particular groups who typically get left out, or who appear uninterested in taking part? In some areas, there appear to have been spontaneous efforts to engage with more marginalised groups of young people, but the international review team heard little of more systematic or structured approaches to ensuring that a "participatory offer" is universally available and, if desired, accessible. It could be argued that the youth population falls into four broad groups in relation to the challenge of youth participation: those who know about and take the opportunities, those who know about but decline the opportunities, those who are unaware of the opportunities, but open to them and those for whom such opportunities do not exist. It is important to differentiate both "youth" and "reach". The most vulnerable young people (such as the Roma youth in Shkodra) may be less interested in participation per se and more interested in more concrete opportunities. This perspective would be consistent with Maslow's hierarchy of needs, but it should not preclude the existence of a participatory offer.

Second, much of what is described as youth participation seems to be focused on dedicated practical activities, rather than more abstract advocacy for children and young people's rights. Again, there is nothing inherently wrong with this, so long as the latter possibilities are available to those participating in the formal structures (children's government and youth parliaments in particular) rather than proscribed. There can be a counter-participatory effect if young people's energy is channelled solely into practical action.

Third, now that the input of participating young people is reasonably well embedded, there will be increasing attention to impact and outcomes arising from that contribution. One respondent captured this issue rather well:

> There is a general view that the demographics of Albania, where young people are more prevalent than anywhere else in Europe except Kosovo, mean that there should be significant investment in youth. Young people themselves are increasingly involved in advocacy and lobbying, "but nobody is listening to us".

The so-called "empowerment" of young people could well backfire if there is no evidence that their voice is taken seriously. As many respondents testified, there was until very recently an overwhelming lack of confidence amongst young people about their capacity to create change; there were huge cultural obstacles to youth activism and participation. Young people did not believe they could make a difference and "had a passive approach to life". This mentality is still present in many young people but "there is much more evidence showing young people's self-belief". It would be foolish to destroy it once again. Not that young people anticipate that all their wishes are going to be fulfilled but – as in Fier – they need to see that their contribution and their efforts have been given sensible and serious consideration.

Fourth, as with any youth participatory structures anywhere, there is the question of sustainability and renewal, which cannot simply be left to chance. Mechanisms have to be put in place to ensure what might be called "rolling" entry and exit procedures, if vacuums are to be avoided. There are numerous models available for achieving this, but it is usually dependent on effective co-ordination by a facilitator, such as the Youth Parliament co-ordinator in Durrës or the youth centre worker in Fier.

Fifth, now that various democratic structures for youth participation have been established in Albania, some consideration may need to be given to the case for categorical structures. These would be directed at specific categories of young people, towards whom particular elements of youth policy may be directed. We are thinking here about, for example, early school drop-outs, Roma and Egyptian youth, young people with disabilities, or young people in remote rural areas. Dedicated platforms for consultation and discussion with these groups may sometimes be more important for effective youth policy development than more conventional democratic arrangements, however much the latter have particular relevance and significance in the new Albania.

Finally, there is an argument that some aspects of child and youth participation have now "come of age" and need to be detached from their origins in the international NGO community and more firmly and formally embedded in public institutional arrangements. This may still be a premature suggestion because the international review team was told that some structures and procedures remain precarious but, if the public administration is as committed to youth participation as the rhetoric of the National Youth Strategy proclaims (and given its contribution to date, it should be), then its stability can only be assured through some stronger guarantees from the public authorities.

---

**Recommendation 18**

*The framework for youth participation that has been established in Albania is impressive. There appears to be real commitment to this issue and youth NGOs, with some serious support from international donors, have worked hard on implementation. There are weaknesses in most of the structures, however, which do require attention. Conceptually, the rationale was rarely articulated, beyond the UNCRC, though there are many other reasons for supporting youth participation. Operationally, there were issues about what young people actually did, what they said, who they said it to and what the results were. There are some exemplary stories, but the whole architecture of youth participation now needs cementing into a stronger infrastructure.*

# 4. issues identified by the international review team

## Youth information

> In a country like Albania where propaganda and a stranglehold on information had existed for nearly 50 years, thinking in stereotypes was to be expected. ... Regional prejudice was entrenched; the image of the north as the centre of backwardness had been a longstanding feature of "common knowledge" with southerners dispatched to northern villages to teach them civilised ways. (De Waal 2007, p. 35)

One of the first objectives of the reformed National Youth Council is to establish an information centre for young people, with information points in the 12 regions (prefectures). This is also a potential central role for the proposed National Youth Centre. The question that then always presents itself, however, is what kind of information and how is it to be communicated? Many young people still have relatively limited access to the Internet; though most schools are connected to the Internet, the international review team was told by some young people that points and moments for access can be heavily restricted and regulated. According to the Institute for Development of Research and Alternatives (2008) around two fifths of boys and well over half of girls do not use the Internet. Members of various participatory structures talked at some length about the worsening "digital divide":

> We are in the capital and most of us have at least one computer in our families. But go to the countryside and the story is very different. And given that the computer is the main source of information these days, then this is increasing the divide between the city and the country. And we can't physically take the information to the north or the south because we also have other responsibilities in our lives. There are Internet cafes but some young women are not allowed to go to them. Yes, schools do sometimes have fancy equipment, but sometimes there are no chairs and sometimes the rooms are locked. Some students do complain about their lack of access to the Internet and lack of access to rooms with computers. Other students do have the possibility of accessing information but they lack the motivation to do so because of the culture and the institutions around them. We need new culture and new inspiration!

New information and communication technologies may therefore also have to be supplemented by more traditional forms of disseminating information: leaflets, posters, magazines, word of mouth, through schools and possibly television. Indeed, the Youth Ministry makes commercials for both public and private TV to publicise and report on every project it supports and to encourage the involvement of youth NGOs, but – contrary to the points raised above – it argued that young people's access to the Internet was "not a problem any more", now that there were computers in every school. It is, in fact, very difficult to get an accurate sense of young people's access to and usage of the Internet (two very different things, of course). The young people in Bushat said that they did not have computers at home but there was no problem using them at school and, alternatively, they could go to an Internet café. In the poor environment of the Roma community centre in Shkodra, a young man handed the rapporteur for the international review team a memory stick to transfer some rap music by Noizy. The youth NGO Beyond the Barriers offers training courses in computers for young people with disabilities.

The approach taken to information provision has to depend, of course, on what the goal is: information for understanding (about, for example, the law, or the risks of drug taking), information for action and engagement (about, for example, campaigns or youth parliaments) or information for behaviour change (about, for example, incentives and penalties around school attendance or criminal behaviour). It is now well established in other parts of Europe that "youth information" is a process and a practice within youth work, not just a technical exercise. Too often, the international review team simply heard calls for "more information" without any real explication about what sort of information was required, where it needed to be directed, how it should or could be used, and who was likely to access it. There might be merits in thinking through the concept of "FREUD in a human envelope",[28] an idea developed by a group of very clever young people attending a "student forum" in Prague in 1999. The "human envelope" would be the sort of professional practitioners whom the international review team met in Fier.

Most children in Albania know very little or nothing about the Internet, computers, drug prevention, Aids prevention and sexual relationships, though two thirds of children know something about children's rights. More girls than boys, those in school rather than those not in school, and urban rather than rural children knew about children's rights, particular the right to education (four fifths of children), the right to free expression, the right to play and the right not to be mistreated or hurt (around half of all children) (Institute for Development of Research and Alternatives 2008, p. 158).

---

28. FREUD is an acronym standing for Find, Retrieve, Evaluate, Use and Defend. The "human envelope" is the educator enabling young people to apply this process to the proliferation of information that is now, at least theoretically, available to them. What is evidence-based? What is marketing or advertising? What is just populist propaganda or bland statement based on prejudice or stereotypes? Young people are rarely short of information; it is what they access and how they handle it that is important.

One international NGO conceded that Internet access and use was still relatively limited but maintained that "the seeds of information are being sown, which must be a good thing". The Open Society Institute now houses a low-cost or no-cost computer area and a meeting space for youth NGOs (called "the NGO house"), but disappointment was expressed about its take-up, despite the fact that charges for the meeting space are around 10% of the cost of hiring room in a hotel (apparently the other alternative in Tirana). The reason given for underuse was the location ("we are a bit out of the way", though this seemed to be a tame excuse: the international review team walked there in a short time) and the fact that there has been a lot of building work going on (which we also considered to be a strange explanation if NGOs are really in need of such a facility, which they claim to be). The Open Society Institute should nevertheless be complimented on its commitment to this provision:

> The public universities have set up centres for student information, which is an important development. We want to convey that information is a fundamental issue in a society such as this, but we need to do a much better job. Those that have used the NGO house tend to be those that have received grants from us, and sometimes we build that into contracts in order to keep costs down.

Save the Children agreed that information remained a big challenge, suggesting that even if children's governments are assured by law, "this still doesn't always mean that it is really happening on the ground": "Children lack information, even if they have the right to a voice, the right to participate."

Strangely, there was little mention by young people themselves of their own need for information. They obviously either felt that they had access to sources of information or were blissfully ignorant! This raises the issue of the balance to be struck between "proactive" and "reactive" information provision. It is one thing to respond to requests by young people for information (on issues such as careers prospects, studying abroad, or local youth projects) and another thing to decide on core information needs of young people, whether they request it or not. The transmission of information takes place, therefore, in a kind of vertical and horizontal matrix. Youth NGOs seemed to see the "solution" to information deficiencies as being better laws from the top and better information on the way down. This is probably a misguided, if comforting delusion and our analysis of the law (above) does not provide a great deal of reassurance that this is likely to happen. Yet, despite repeated insinuations of communication breakdown and information failure at many levels, the youth NGOs – or at least the small group of youth NGOs who met the international review team on a number of occasions – appear to have effective strands of communication. Whatever the merits of this (in terms of sharing good practice, identifying funding sources and supporting training and projects), the international review team would express two concerns. The first is that the current system seems to rely too heavily on personal contacts, raising questions about the sustainability of these platforms of communication when people move on. The second is the more speculative thought that current arrangements may have produced something of an exclusive "club" from which newcomers in the youth NGO sector may be de facto excluded (or at least feel excluded); a more structured approach to information-sharing and communication channels is probably desirable to counter such perceptions or suspicions. Both Partners Albania and the revitalised National Youth Council clearly have a prospective central role to play on this particular front.

Finally, there is the information platform relating to awareness-raising and campaigns, not all of which may find favour with the government and the public administrations, since they may be inherently critical of them. One example might include the "Life" campaign being supported by UNICEF. This relates to the official smoking ban that one respondent described as "100% unimplementation"! The campaign is being orchestrated by a youth NGO. Another example might be the Durrës Youth Parliament's co-ordination of a petition against development at Porto Romano. There will, no doubt, be other even more contentious issues in the future.

There are, then, at least three forms of information provision that demand more concerted and systematic attention. Greater thought needs to be given to the content and method used for information directed towards young people, as well as that requested by young people. More structured systems for information-sharing between those working in the youth field are required. And, where the public authorities are not likely to support information for campaigns directed at their own deficiencies, more thought ought to be given to the strategic alliances that should be struck for effective information and communication on specific issues.[29]

---

**Recommendation 19**

*General calls for 'better information' suggest an absence of a more calibrated understanding of the role of information in youth policy – both for youth professionals and for young people. The international review team believes that more structured and focused information systems are required for both constituencies but, before these are developed, more clarity of thought is required about their objectives, audiences and methodologies.*

---

## Leisure, culture, sports and non-formal learning

"We village children, spend our time either reading or doing house work. ... In the future, if the commune (local government) invests money, we will have a movie centre in our village." (village high-school boy, aged 16, Synej)

---

29. This point was reinforced by comments made at the national hearing, which wanted less argument and dissent amongst youth NGOs and others and more commitment to information-sharing and mutual support.

"These days many of us do not understand that entertainment is not only the coffee bars and that the sports activities can be a lot of fun, especially when you do those with the people you enjoy being with, like your friends." (compulsory-school girl, aged 11, Korca)

(Institute for Development of Research and Alternatives 2008, p. 86)

One of the casualties of post-communist life now that there are no co-operatives or Houses of Culture for get-togethers, is intensive community interaction. ... The young feel the loss of companionship severely. (De Waal 2007, p. 100)

Village life now that co-operatives and houses of culture no longer function is particularly solitary and bleak for young girls who no longer attend school. (De Waal 2007, p. 102)

During the 1990s, Albania experienced a progressive appropriation of green areas and youth recreation spaces – such as youth centres, community libraries, parks and playgrounds. The transformation of these public spaces into private holdings brought about a massive use of concrete, as well as the disappearance of the majority of places where children and young people could play games, practise sports or simply pass their free time. (Ministry of Tourism, Culture, Youth and Sports 2006, p. 37)

The National Youth Strategy (p. 39) is committed to the "reappropriation of public spaces usurped during the transition period and the creation of youth centres and community libraries throughout the country". Yet, strangely, following its discussion of "Free time, sports and culture" in its Situation Analysis and after setting out the points above within its Vision, Priorities and Strategic Goals, the National Youth Strategy says absolutely nothing about this theme in its section on Policies. This is quite bizarre and a sufficient source of concern for the international review team to elect to identify this theme as one of its key youth policy areas.[30]

The difficulty for the international review team was that it received relatively little substantive evidence about young people's use of "free time". The ministry suggested that young people went to "bars, clubs, movies and the gym". They walked around and went for coffee. And there were free cultural activities available, and activities and concerts and "other possibilities" organised by NGOs. But this was a portrait of what goes on in Tirana: "we want to extend this to other places in Albania". Young people themselves often said that they had little free time for their own autonomous leisure pursuits. They were either involved in studying, working or structured projects. There is, of course, a chicken-and-egg issue here: if there are fewer leisure-time opportunities these days (as many respondents suggested) then young people clearly cannot be engaged in them. Few respondents

---

30. There was some consensus about the need for more joint effort towards common goals. One individual said that "we need more transparency and debate, not attack and criticism".

seemed to understand questions about "associational life", social activities that connected young people and adults, and non-formal learning leisure possibilities. One response to such a question was as follows:

> No, there is not much going on. The cities here in Albania are small. There's not enough volume business, so cinemas get closed. Girls have to be in at home by seven or eight in the evening. There's lots of recreational activities during the day, but not much in the evenings; commercially or socially. And some cities are quite divided, for various reasons.

The perspective was corroborated during our visit to Fier:

> There is very little social activity for young people in Fier. No cinema, although there is a theatre. No sports facilities, because old sites have all been built on. So there is nothing for young people to do. There is some commercial provision and obviously bars and cafés, but this has a terrible effect on young people: they just drink coffee for amusement, not learning, there is nothing to learn.

This was a common theme in commentaries: the corrosive effects of café culture, compared with the wholesome and educational benefits of youth participation and involvement in projects. Blanket condemnation of "sitting around in coffee bars" appears to be an almost obligatory remark in any discussion of the changes in the ways young people use their "'leisure".

Constructive use of leisure was almost always equated with engagement in sports or supplementary learning possibilities in the realms of languages, music and art. In Shkodra, the mayor was emphatic about his commitment to "forming more civilised leisure-time activities for children". He illustrated this by describing co-operation with the university and planned visits to Brussels and Strasbourg. Purposeful leisure-time activity for young people was linked to supporting a group of girls to organise activities, and holding dedicated Youth Days and Children's Days in which children and young people were able to showcase their musical, artistic and dance abilities. Shkodra had tried to create these "spaces" for young people, maintaining that "the most important aspect of these activities is the cultivation of a new mentality amongst young people and the wider population" – a spirit of initiative, enterprise and achievement. The mayor listed a range of projects involving young people that were currently going on in Shkodra, supported from a range of sources, including the municipality and the regional directorate.

Sport figured prominently in the leisure interests of young people, notably boys. In Bushat, the absence of boys from the meeting with the international review team was because they were taking part in a sports competition at school. Indeed, much of young people's leisure-time seemed to be spent in the school (where young people participated in competitions in, for example, literature or chemistry), or involved in activities such as "touristic" visits and going to the cinema. The boys were more focused on football and basketball; on their behalf, the girls reported the damaged soccer pitch and asked what the mayor was going to do about it! In reply, the mayor said there were plans for an indoor sports palace, but the funding had yet to be secured. This had, apparently, been a long-standing promise. The girls themselves said they hoped to get a library.

The young people in Durrës said that "there was not a lot of choice for entertainment, just private leisure clubs". They reported that there had once been a cinema, but this was now closed. Hence, in their view, the importance of the youth centre when it had existed:

> The space was important because there need to be opportunities, especially for more marginalised groups, for young people to be able to spend time, do things, exchange views with others, receive information, avoid being involved in more negative phenomena. ... Otherwise they have just school. Before the youth centre was closed, there were vocational courses free of charge, activities for those with talents, capacity-building activities, funded by an Italian NGO for three years (but in fact only two years).

Because of the preoccupation with, and commitment to education on the part of most young people in Albania (contrary to their hypothesis, Orgocka and Jovanovic (2006, p. 273) found that "Albanian youths are focused on exploration and commitment to education and occupation"), leisure-time activities organised by youth NGOs usually take place on weekends. In part, this is also to accommodate young women who, for historical and cultural reasons, are not allowed to be outside after dark.

The international review team's understanding of sports provision in Albania remained limited, despite the fact that the Youth Ministry is also responsible for sport. We did not learn about the costs that might be associated with participation in sport. Some members of the international review team did, however, visit a sports' NGO which appeared to be more like a fitness club. It was also somewhat like a neighbourhood gym, run by a teacher who also works in a school and some instructors who teach volleyball, gymnastics and dance in schools. Young people can come to the fitness club and exercise there too – for free. Costs are paid for by the ministry. The venue also prepares young people for competitions. Its revenue is topped up by commercial activities. People cannot just walk in from the street; they come after discussion and negotiation with the instructors. It was emphatic, however, that it was "not just for the best kids" – it was also for self-improvement. The international review team was told that all schools in Tirana are covered by similar fitness centres supported by the ministry. There are, nevertheless, residual questions regarding the eligibility criteria for gaining access and admission and young people's awareness of the existence of such provision – an information question. During the visit by the international review team, only one young person was present; just down the road was a commercial fitness centre and it was full.

Youth festivals seem to be important in today's Albania. They were discussed in Tirana, Durrës and Shkodra. The inclusive nature of such events was challenged and is apparently controversial. Even though young Roma people in Shkodra do participate, they do not want to be performing and perceived as members of the Roma community, but rather integrated alongside other young people. They want their competence to be recognised as individuals, not as Roma. Yet this stance is part of a broader paradox we encountered with young Roma people: they seek integration but also seek the retention of their cultural identities. The work with young people by the Roma community centre in Tirana appears to be making inroads in addressing this position.

The strange thing about this focus on the leisure activities of young people is that – for men of all ages – leisure-time is very visibly spent in public space. There are numerous pool halls, and chess and dominoes are to be seen everywhere in the parks and on the streets. But such activity is clearly governed, in cultural terms, by gender and increasingly by age: we saw few young people, though we did see a small child wielding a pool cue at a table that was higher than him!

It is such associational space that appears to be denied to the young. This may hardly be an issue for young people themselves, probably because they are likely to be unaware of the possibilities this might offer, but it is still an issue for the international review team. The youth centres we heard about were generally office and meeting spaces rather than rooms specifically for associations. Spending time together, with professionally supportive adults, is a critical catalyst for personal development and subsequent engagement with, and attachment to, civil society. It may involve the development, planning and implementation of projects, but it may not. There may be a strong commitment to at least the concept of youth participation (see above), but its development has tended to channel young people's energies in project design and delivery around (usually) relatively non-controversial and apolitical themes. Activities are part of the repertoire of youth work, but association is the central plank of "non-formal learning", a term that was hardly mentioned during our visits and certainly not understood. There were isolated glimpses of both understanding and non-formal educational practice, but they were few and far between. Without a base where young people can experience association, activities, action, advice and access (Department of Education and Science 1982) through reasonably autonomous decision-making, the rhetoric of "participation and empowerment" is diluted. There are, of course, many different traditions of "youth work" across Europe (see Coussée 2008, Verschelden et al. 2009) but, increasingly, with the need to engender personal confidence, competence, motivation and initiative in young people, non-formal educational practices are coming to be regarded as a key component of young people's learning and development, both for the labour market and engagement with civil society.

---

**Recommendation 20**

*New technologies do offer alternative possibilities for young people to communicate and network. However, there remains a strong case for some dedicated physical space at the local level where young people can gather – associate – and engage in or plan activities as well as simply "hang around", talk and enjoy themselves. Such space is ideally sheltered – and therefore buildings are desirable – but alternatives such as sports fields (or the corners of them!) or outdoor seating areas with an optional bad weather cover, rather like the ubiquitous car washing spaces, would be another possibility.*

## Youth crime and justice

> The prevention of youth crime is a big issue. We have only just started developing programmes to try to do this. We have a new probation service, which will work closely with NGOs. Education is the important thing. The opening of a school means the closing of a prison. We need more early intervention. Until now, we have given too much attention to dealing with the effects, not with the cause. We need to deal with children and young people who break the law before they become formed in that way as adults. (Ministry of Justice)

The international review team concludes its three selected youth policy domains with a focus on youth crime and justice. In some respects, this arena is an exemplar of what clear thinking, an orchestrated campaign, the engagement of significant others and – obviously – the securing of the necessary resources can achieve over a relatively short space of time. The implementation is, admittedly, in very early days (the international review team's visit to the new youth correctional, or "re-integration" centre at Kavaja took place in the afternoon of only its second day of operation) and there are still key aspirations to be fulfilled, an outdated system has already been transformed and the direction of travel is impressive.

Paradoxically, though Albania has an internationally negative reputation for its "big crime" (corruption, money laundering and trafficking in drugs and human beings), the international review team did not hear concerns about crime (and certainly not youth crime) from young people themselves, and "youth as a problem" was not part of the dialogue with professionals, as it so often is in other countries. Even the young people "on the street" appeared to be more entrepreneurial than troublesome, trying to sell us pens and, on a day when it was pouring with rain, umbrellas! The young Roma people in Shkodra said that they had never had any encounters with the law on account of illegal or anti-social behaviour. The Ministry of Justice reported, however, that typical forms of youth offending in Albania were car theft, petty shoplifting and drug-related crimes (dealing and offences committed in order to finance personal drugs habits). The international review team had expressly asked to meet with police officers during its second visit but, disappointingly, this did not take place. As a result, the perspectives expressed below are inevitably partial and may be considered by some to offer a somewhat distorted account. Nevertheless, we believe there are still some important messages to convey.

The National Youth Strategy (p. 29) acknowledges that the involvement of young people in criminal activities remains "at very low levels", although it suggests that this has been increasing in recent years. The "situation analysis" further suggests that a weakness in the Albanian criminal justice system is the lack of a "proper legal and institutional framework" for young offenders and an absence of effective collaboration between penal institutions and other relevant agencies: social services, schools, justice entities, the family or the community. The vision expressed within the National Youth Strategy includes improvements in preventative work and the development of alternative measures of punishment.

Furthermore, the Youth Ministry commits itself, in collaboration with the Ministry of Justice, to engagement in a process for the creation of a "legal package for the young" (formally, the Legal Reform Package on Minors).

In fact, the reform of youth justice started some four years ago at the instigation of UNICEF. Its vision was the modernisation, in relation to juveniles (those aged between 14, the age of criminal responsibility – though it is 16 for minor offences or "misdemeanours" – and 18), of a criminal justice system that was described as "very punitive and not at all proportionate". Severe measures had previously been "the only response" and there was no discussion of approaches to youth crime prevention. Though the penal code allowed for alternatives to institutional custody (such as imprisonment), there had been no implementation; as a result, the choice for the police and the courts when young offenders were apprehended was, put simply, to lock them up or let them go. Since then, however, there have been significant developments: the formation of a probation service from 2008 dealing with parole, community supervision and mediation; free legal assistance; the extension of alternatives to detention; the establishment of restorative justice approaches for first-time offenders; and the construction of a new detention institution for 40 young offenders. UNICEF was clearly delighted at such developments:

> We had a campaign concerning the administration of juvenile justice, promoting alternatives and advocating prevention. We focused on how to address the issue of youth delinquency, seeing the offender as both a perpetrator and as a victim. There have been lots of results: legislation, a broader range of provision, a probation service, community service, offender mediation ... So this has brought about a big change in the system. These have been major developments from the very punitive former system. There has been a great deal of progress.

Not only do such reforms improve the effectiveness (and reduce the costs) of the way the criminal justice system deals with young people (and adult offenders, too), there will be wider social benefits and stronger compliance with international human rights expectations, as a recent Organization for Security and Co-operation in Europe (OSCE) Evaluation Report on the introduction of Probation in Albania made clear:

> In this way, the society will benefit from more appropriate treatment of offenders, leading to lower rates of recidivism in the future. Fewer offenders are expected to be remanded in custody awaiting trial or sentence. Social inclusion will be promoted, by reducing the social exclusion of offenders. At the same time, the compliance with Albania's human rights obligations will be enhanced through improvement of treatment of offenders, especially minors, women and ethnic minority groups. (OSCE 2009, p. 4)

For young people below the age of criminal responsibility (under 14 for crimes, under 16 for misdemeanours) the law provides only for the imposition of "educational measures" but this relates to facilities that no longer exist. This produces distinct challenges for preventative programmes, but there are models that address such challenges elsewhere in Europe that could be considered by the Albanian authorities. For young people who do appear before the criminal courts, there has been progress arising from the establishment of special sections of trial courts dedicated exclusively to dealing with juvenile offenders. The appointment of judges who specialise in such cases has arguably improved the quality of justice meted out to and experienced by young offenders. Juveniles facing trial in the courts have the right to social, legal and psychological assistance during the criminal justice process.

Responsibility for all correctional and detention facilities, the former in 1993-94 and the latter in 2005-07, has been transferred from the Ministry of the Interior to the Ministry of Justice. The Law on the Rights and Treatment of Prisoners stipulates that young offenders should serve their sentences (usually half of the tariff that would be imposed on an adult, to a maximum of 12.5 years) in specially designed establishments or in separate units of other correctional institutions. However, until the opening of the youth correctional facility at Kavaja in November 2009 (see below), no such separate provision existed. However, those on remand (pre-trial detention) will continue to be held in police stations or adult prisons, albeit separately. Young offenders can only be questioned in the presence of a lawyer, parent or psychological expert.

The OSCE report concludes its discussion of the criminal justice system as it affects young offenders in Albania with the following remarks:

> Unfortunately, the Albanian legislation doesn't provide for any specific alternatives to imprisonment that can be imposed on children who commit crimes, based on their personality, needs, vulnerability, maturity, etc. ... [W]e can say that some steps have been made in bringing Albanian law and practice into conformity with international standards and best practices regarding juvenile offenders. Still, much remains to be done, especially regarding the legal framework for children who commit crimes. (OSCE 2009, p. 15)

The OSCE report makes some specific recommendations with which the international review team wholly concurs: the need to reduce the delays in investigation and adjudication of juvenile cases; reducing the use of pre-trial detention and increasing the use of diversion in appropriate cases; establishing measures to deal with children under the age of 14 who commit offences; and ensuring the proper training of the staff who have direct contact with young offenders.

Since that report, some small steps have been made in these directions, such as the introduction of restorative justice procedures, supported by NGOs, for relatively minor offences, in which mediation and reparation are viewed as an appropriate response. One huge step has also been taken – the building and opening of the dedicated custodial facility (youth re-education centre) at Kavaja. Located 60 km south of Tirana, it houses 40 convicted juveniles in four units, described by UNICEF as "a family-like organisation of the premises". It is modelled on an institution in Austria and was financed by funds from the European Union. Not including the 36 custody officers (guards), there are 34 staff: social workers, psychologists, educators, vocational training instructors, doctors and dentists. Experts from the Netherlands helped to design the regime, and the rules and procedures governing the prison's operation. The staff have been trained and have gathered experience through placements in other custodial institutions and by working with the young people prior to their transfer to Kavaja.

There were just 13 young people at Kavaja when members of the international review team paid a visit. Their ages ranged from 14 to 18 and their offences were serious: murder, assault, theft, and possession of narcotics and illegal weapons. There is a clear procedure for admission, assessment and then allocation to one of the four wings, according to recommendations – based on written information available and a face-to-face meeting with the individual concerned – made to the director by a commission of the professional staff.

The regime itself is underpinned by a system of rewards and sanctions, the former being things such as the length of phone calls allowed, more time with families during visits and a greater frequency of visits. The custody officers do wear police uniforms but they are "quite soft". A typical day was described:

07.00 Get up sharp
Breakfast
09.00 Education activity and outdoor association until 12.30
13.00 Lunch and recreation
14.00 Education
18.30/19.00 Dinner
Association in each section's communal hall
21.00 Bedtime

We were not surprised to hear that there had been "no problems so far", with the first "residents" having only arrived the previous day, though the staff team had been in place for a month. The staff seemed very young and the director confirmed that many were new graduates. The international review team felt their reasons for seeking employment at Kavaja seemed a strange blend of real motivation to make a difference and some level of naivety about the challenges they were likely to face. They spoke of the "social and human dimension" of the work they would be doing. One older recruit said that, being a mother, she would have a similar role for the young people at the institution. One of the young recruits made the following comment:

> I am not so far from the age of those detained here and I was very much attached to sports activities myself, so by mingling together the learning from university with personal experiences and motivation, I thought it would be good to apply.

Another remarked that he hoped to effect change in the young people "by being helpful and friendly", adding astutely that he wanted to establish close engagement with this age group because they were going through a range of common problems that face all teenagers as well as the specific issues they face. His focus, he said, almost providing the sound-bite for the establishment, was "to lend a hand, to try to pull them out". A newly appointed psychologist was more circumspect about her motivation but said that prisons were laboratories, presenting a "good opportunity and challenge" for the kind of work she had trained for.

Research had suggested that around 35-40 spaces were the likely number needed in Albania for the "category" of young person that the Kavaja establishment was designed to cater for. The shift patterns for custody officers (guards) had been drawn from a scheme witnessed in the Netherlands. On each of the four wings, three tutors were routinely supported by just one uniformed custody officer (though of course more were on duty elsewhere in the prison).

When asked whether the staff considered themselves to be pioneers at the "heavy" end of youth justice in Albania, the answer was cautious, but there was unanimity that this was something very new and that they were "treading new ground". Beyond the training that staff had already received, it was anticipated that further training and study visits would take place.

We had a tour of the prison, where we asked about issues such as visiting protocols, smoking, how young people could acquire resources for things like soap and telephone calls (they cannot earn money at Kavaja because Albanian law does not allow the imposition of work on minors), reception procedures, education, health care (especially for those more "at risk" of self-harm because of mental health difficulties) and recreation and association.

There are education classrooms, with seating for young people from one section (that is, 10 young people). Teachers come in from outside to teach the current curriculum (this is on top of the educators who are part of the 34 professional staff). These outside teachers can provide certificates, which give no indication of where the certification was acquired (that is, without the stamp of the institution). On the same floor are rooms for storing materials for the social care and education staff. Further along is the infirmary and the doctor's room. It is hoped that UNICEF will provide some of the equipment needed for these rooms. There are three dedicated "observation rooms" for at-risk young people elsewhere in the institution; these are used mainly for young people on arrival, who are subject to special monitoring during their first three days.

There is a library with four modern Samsung computers (but even supervised access to the Internet is strictly forbidden by prison department rules), though these will soon be moved elsewhere to make the library into a proper "reading room". Currently, however, there is not much else in there, except a booklet on youth rights and four short novels by a celebrated prisoner doing a life sentence in Albania. UNICEF is committed to providing some 300 books for the library.

Downstairs, there is a hall and an outdoor "airing" place. The hall is, at present, a large empty space though, it is hoped, it will become the place and space for a pool table, table tennis, performances and general association. The outdoor "airing" place is a narrow strip with a large "cage" (exercise yard) where fresh air can be enjoyed. Each of the four sections has identical provision.

Seven of the 13 young people who are already at Kavaja were on the wing we visited. Those we met were engaging, with smiles on their faces and a willingness to talk: they felt that the place was OK, certainly better than anywhere else they had been. They still had aspirations and dreams: to be a mason, an actor, a businessman and a musician. The "social" room had a decent sized colour TV and two round tables with four chairs surrounding each. There was a small office, and a couple of rooms, one of which was a "counselling room". Through a locked door were the five cells, for double up (two in each): these were a very decent size, with windows that open and let the fresh air in, two small wardrobes for clothes, and a toilet and wash basin with a shutting door. (It will be interesting to see what they do when they get their first cases of self-harming, violence in the toilet, or faeces thrown out of the windows – all relatively common events in young offender institutions). At the end of the corridor is a single "punishment" room for miscreant lads and the shower unit. Everything was very new and very impressive.

The lads commented favourably on the way they were treated by the staff and rather self-critically conceded that they themselves often behaved worse. They clearly valued the positive relationships with the staff. Later, some staff said that it was important to make "every day a different day" and some worked extra time (especially on weekends) and "went the extra mile". Good relationships had sometimes been forged through contact before these young men had arrived here at Kavaja.

The re-education or reintegration centre at Kavaja cost €1.78 million.[31] It is located adjacent to residential housing and so is very much an "institution in the community". There have even been some efforts at contact, communication and integration with local residents (through collecting water from them as if there had been a breakdown in the supply to the prison) and welcoming interest from neighbours. The building, from a distance, looks like a modern college or even an art hotel. You have to get close to see the high wire fencing.

It is very impressive and the built design provides every enabling opportunity for the best practice to develop. The director appears to be a charismatic, engaging and committed individual who had worked at the Ministry of Justice and has only been in this job for seven months. The international review team wishes him and his staff the very best in their endeavours as pioneers of youth justice in Albania. Yet the international review team also noted that it will be interesting to see how quickly the fabric deteriorates (the bare walls will soon get covered, if not with posters, then with scratches) and how quickly the evident motivation and commitment of the staff fades as they meet the inevitable challenges of the place. Of course, we hope this does not happen. The establishment at Kavaja could turn into a flagship – an oasis of innovation in a desert of youth justice policy across many other parts of Europe!

More generally, youth justice in Albania is a sector of youth policy where there has clearly been significant progress during the past few years, and it would be

---

31. An equivalent-sized custodial institution for juveniles in the UK would probably now cost between £30 million and £50 million.

remiss of the international review team not to pay its compliments to the energies and efforts of the NGOs, government departments and international partners that have made this happen. There has been real implementation and even broader aspiration. The latter now needs more attention to produce further implementation, especially in the areas of preventative work with children under the age of 14, community supervision for those aged between 14 and 18, pre-trial detention for the same age group and training for those who are going to work with these young people. Even practitioners who have acquired the general skills in their field need particular specialities – around, for example, anger management, depression, loss, incident de-escalation, and physical control – if they are to be effective practitioners with young offenders, especially those at the "harder" end of the spectrum. There should also be additional focus on the question of follow-up and after-care. What happens to these young people when they are released into the community from places such as the institution at Kavaja? If they are serving long sentences, they will be moved to adult prisons and perhaps all the constructive work performed at Kavaja will rapidly unravel. There is already a very progressive analysis of what is needed for young offenders in Albania; there now needs to be consolidation of the new developments that have already been effected and further practical implementation on the ground.

---

**Recommendation 21**

*The international review team strongly recommends the further development of community-based provision for young offenders – for both supervision and surveillance – as an alternative to custody, a platform for restorative justice and as a mechanism for rehabilitation and re-integration.*

↑ issues identified by the international review team

# Conclusion

## A critical reflection

The international review team felt that there was much to compliment in both the strategic vision for young people in Albania (enshrined in the National Youth Strategy) and in the practical action undertaken by the many youth NGOs we met and in the municipalities we visited. Passion, vision and commitment were certainly not in short supply, though the bridge between policy intentions and operational implementation often appeared to be missing. NGOs sometimes got on with their work despite, rather than because of the governmental framework. Ministries churned out strategies, laws and action plans often quite oblivious of what was taking place elsewhere, whatever the claims were for inter-ministerial communication, consultation and collaboration.

The National Youth Strategy does provide a well-constructed and coherent youth policy framework. It sets out, on a range of pertinent youth policy issues, analyses of the current situation, a vision with accompanying priorities and goals, policy proposals and ideas for monitoring and evaluation. There is a strong will to promote youth participation and to design transversal, inter-sectoral policies for young people. However – and it is a big "but" – such a framework, with some relatively minor adaptation, could have been written for virtually any other country: the issues are generally prominent ones for youth policy anywhere, even if the detail, balance and challenge may be different. In that sense, the policy framework remains rather, literally, abstract: disconnected from some of the tough political, economic and social realities that prevail in Albania.

It may be useful at this point to note that youth policy variation between countries is often less a question of substantive differences in the main priorities and more a consequence of differences in political will and available resources. Albania's aspirations for its young people, articulated in the National Youth Strategy, cannot be faulted; its capacity to deliver across this spectrum of themes, and throughout the country, is quite another matter. The policies proposed make absolute sense in relation to the preceding analysis and vision, but "what to do" is one thing, "how to do it" is quite another. Recurrently, the international review team was told that there were laws that were not implemented or that nobody observed. This gap between the theory of policy and the practice of policy is typical for these kinds of abstract blueprint approaches. Policies are not achieved through the writing of a document! There can, of course, be "natural" resistance to centralised attempts to find and impose solutions to social questions, particularly in countries with certain histories, like Albania. People are inclined not to "fit in" with new prescriptions. The National Youth Strategy itself concedes that "initiatives to transform the youth sector and youth reality tend to stay on a theoretical level".

Another scenario, however, the antithesis of an abstract "blueprint approach", is what might be called a concrete "scattergun approach", typical of the support provided by at least some international NGOs that do support real projects and practice but often shift their focus and priorities with limited reference to the work of others in either the donor community, the domestic NGO sector, or the public administration. In the middle of these two positions is the dedicated and concentrated focus on specific youth policy issues, the most obvious examples being the development of youth parliaments and the campaign for the modernisation of youth justice, both supported by UNICEF.

Neither of these latter approaches are inherently wrong, but they do not help to consolidate, and can at times undermine, a general framework for youth policy, born out of a broader societal analysis, proper consultative procedures and decisions made through the democratic process. The international review team believes that the National Youth Strategy needs to take a further step towards producing that kind of general framework, rooted in the real lives, aspirations and experiences (in all their diversity) of young people, for regional and local application and delivery. Currently, the National Youth Strategy provides an almost too general outline of an ideal society but so much appears to be constructed on very western European models, brought to Albania by (usually) well-intentioned social engineers from numerous organisations with their own values and objectives. These now seem to serve, uncritically, across policy domains (such as health, education, vocational training or justice) as the standard or benchmark, almost regardless of Albanian specificities arising from its particular historical, cultural, social and political traditions and transformations. There may have been a time, during the uncertainties and sometimes chaos of the 1990s, when there was little option but to accept whatever was offered, but there is now a mature indigenous body of knowledge and expertise in the youth field and a more stable political and economic environment that should lead to external thinking being used as a platform for the development of a distinctly Albanian youth policy rather than its determinant.

In the synthesis report of earlier international youth policy reviews (Williamson 2002, 2008) there are references to the five Cs (components) and the four, or eight Ds (dynamics) of national youth policies. These provide a simple test of operational activity and momentum for the future.

*The five Cs*

These refer to the following:

> Coverage – geographical areas, social groups, policy domains
> Capacity – structures for delivery with public and NGO sectors
> Competence – the professional knowledge and skills available
> Co-ordination – communication/collaboration by youth field actors
> Cost – human and financial resources available

We do not intend to dwell for long on these points, for observations have already been made in relation to them. Suffice it to say that the international review team understands the pressure on resources (cost) and any other criticisms must always be pitched against this. Nevertheless, coverage appears extremely patchy in relation both to geographical "reach" and to engaging with many social groups of young people, even if the National Youth Strategy projects an impressively comprehensive coverage of youth policy issues. Co-ordination also appears to be rather "hit and miss", contingent on personal links and contact rather than on structural arrangements. That some other ministries, also dealing in part with youth issues, appeared ignorant or ill-informed of the National Youth Strategy bears witness to this point. Capacity also remains weak and heavily dependent on the work of youth NGOs in tandem with the specificities of local administrations. In English, there is an expression "where there's a will, there's a way" and there is considerable testimony to this at the local level in Albania. But the converse also applies and there are plenty of obstacles to effective implementation that can serve as poor excuses rather than legitimate explanations. Finally, in terms of competence, the international review team was impressed with much of the thinking expressed by respondents during a host of meetings. There may be a shortage of professional expertise, but it is certainly not absent – and this is why the international review team suggests the shaping of a more distinctively Albanian youth policy framework, standing back from western European models and reflecting on their suitability, even if they have been the original source of "new" thinking and understanding in Albania. This may, right now, be difficult in the context of European Union accession, but the international review team is not proposing any rejection of European level standards, just a more realistic, pragmatic and principled adaptation to Albania's context and culture.

*The four, or eight, Ds*

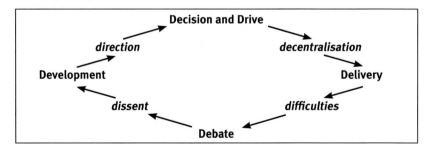

The simple message from this diagram is that youth policy can start or stall at any point in the cycle, for many reasons, such as the innovation or inertia of practice, changing political priorities, or the facilitation or blocking of debate. However, it is a dynamic cycle that needs to be sustained; without any of its components working actively, things will grind to a halt. In Albania, the international review team feels that there is too much weight attached to the far left of the cycle and insufficient consideration given to the right-hand side. Without political championship, of course, any policy initiative is likely to flounder, but unless there are clear strategies for decentralisation, little will reach the ground. Without the evidence from grounded practice, policy thinking remains abstract and there is no basis for refinement, adjustment and development.

The rather abstract nature of the National Youth Strategy is reinforced by a striking absence of data, facts and figures. This is, of course, very problematic if there is a desire to build an evidence-based youth policy framework. The international review team did wonder about "youth research" in Albania and if there was any, who produced it, for what purpose and from which perspectives. We learned little about it, though it is considered by, *inter alia*, the Council of Europe youth policy framework to be a key foundation stone (alongside professional training and the dissemination of good practice) for building informed and effective youth policy. Apparently, in Albania, though there once were youth research organisations, the brain drain has meant that academics with talent have departed elsewhere, and the limited research that is conducted on young people tends to focus on those causing problems (research that is not then published). Consequently, there was therefore a tendency to talk about young people in sweepingly general terms. Moreover, there was largely a focus exclusively on "youth" and "youth issues" rather than a broader question about the relationship of young people with society.

The international review team understands why this may be the case: in former times, the state dictated that relationship. Today, across Europe, there is now the misguided assumption that market forces and the creativity and autonomy of individuals (the "entrepreneurial self") will produce a desirable outcome. But we know this not to be the case (if massive social inequalities and social exclusion are to be avoided or at least mitigated), and all countries have to consider how they want to manage the relationships between people (and especially young people) and society. The goals of youth policy cannot be limited to "positive youth development". This may help young people to find their place in the market but it will not produce social cohesion. This is because opportunities for participation and engagement during their leisure-time tend to be taken by those who already have various social advantages (family life, education, networks) and so those advantages are reinforced, while those further to the margins become relatively even more excluded. The international review team was aware of some of the ad hoc measures taken to engage with more disadvantaged groups (especially in relation to the participation agenda), but more systematic and politically supported approaches are required.

Education, broadly conceived (that is, much more than schooling and universities), lies at the heart of youth policy, and Albanian youth policy, as enshrined in the

National Youth Strategy and as recurrently communicated to us by many respondents, is no exception. All measures are, in some way, "educative", in the sense that they support young people in growing up and growing into adult society. Historically, there have been three established educational milieux[32] and today there is arguably a fourth:

- family: parents, grandparents, brothers, sisters, extended family;
- school and work: teachers, social workers, psychologists, trade unions;
- leisure-time: sports, culture, music, "non-formal" education and youth work;
- media: informal education and "edutainment".

There are always questions to be asked about the relative influence and impact on children and young people of these different milieu and whether or not that influence is consistent across these milieu or contradictory. Clearly there are times when one milieu is non-functional or judged to be inappropriate and alternatives have to be found. This is the role of "social" work, which includes therapeutic social work and child protection but is much broader than that.

The international review team did not get an equal picture of these influences but would wish to note some salient points. With regard to the domain of the family, it is evident that there is a strong family tradition in Albania. Many young people live with their parents until their late 20s. We were therefore especially interested in those young people who, for whatever reason, lacked such family support. The international review team was impressed by the work of SOS Kinderdörfer International and its Children's Village, both in the way it tried to strengthen family support in risk and vulnerable situations and in sustaining support for those youngsters it cared for directly up to the age of 26. This is a solid "child care" policy, one which should provide a model for replication on a broader basis. The vast majority of "at risk" children in Albania (estimated to be around 200 000) currently have no access to anything like this quality of provision.

In the domain of school and work, there is, first, a major concern about the drop-out rate, though a proportion of 20% is not unusual in some other parts of Europe. The causes are unclear, but there is certainly the problem of infrastructure in more remote and rural areas and perhaps a lack of aspiration amongst parents and young people (though the vast majority are deeply committed to education). The relation between aspiration and opportunity can be complex, but motivation to sustain engagement with schooling may be supported by ensuring appropriate and attractive extra-curricular options that are now determined by young people

---

32. These are conceptual distinctions which, in some societies and some communities, may be rather more blurred. Family size and structure clearly affects its influence on socialisation, as does the length of compulsory schooling and the extent to which working life is clearly separated from home life. Such distinctions may be less obvious in some parts of Albania, especially more remote rural areas, where school attendance is less and subsistence farming on domestic plots of land is common.

Conclusion

themselves. There may have to be some more pro-active measures to ensure that those young people at most risk of dropping out have their voice heard on these matters. In relation to work, Albania has a growing economy but, for at least three reasons, an unfavourable position for young people: the extensive informal and black market; the disproportionate number of graduates compared to the number of jobs requiring that level of qualification; and the fact that age, rather than qualification, remains a key factor in seniority. The international review team has not addressed in any detail issues concerning enterprise and entrepreneurship, but a balanced employment strategy (in preparation, according to the National Youth Strategy, p. 23) that includes more attention to regional and local careers, training and employment services is undoubtedly necessary.

Leisure was once described as "the weak link in the chain of socialisation" (when compared with the stronger forces of family, school and work) but it also provides the space for experimentation, exploration and autonomy. It is also the space that can be filled by sports, youth work and non-formal learning. The latter should be considered constructive and valuable in their own right, rather than the mechanisms for "keeping young people away from risky behaviours", which is the starting position in the comments about its value in the National Youth Strategy (p. 39), though then some more positive objectives of such practice are identified:

> As they are key to the cultivation of personal values and principles such as trust, respect, integrity and self-assessment, and to the promotion of positive concepts and social attitudes such as tolerance and team work. (Ministry of Tourism, Culture, Youth and Sports 2006, p. 39)

During both discussions and within the material scrutinised by the international review team, there was scarcely a mention of "youth work" or "non-formal education". About the closest the National Youth Strategy comes to this is in its analysis of the weaknesses around civic education and democratic citizenship during the transition period arising from "the low level of co-operation among policy makers, teachers, parents, the community and civil society groups" (Ministry of Tourism, Culture, Youth and Sports 2006, p. 43). There is also hardly an infrastructure within which to locate such practice, even if the personnel were prepared, because of the decimation of public recreational spaces, open space, or places where young people might gather – spontaneously and informally - for "association". We saw some, and heard about many more projects, but were not aware of structures that might have enabled such potential "youth work" practice. This is an area of youth policy that is of increasing interest at a European level (see Verschelden et al. 2009); the recent youth strategy of the European Commission places "youth work" at the heart of its strategic goals of opportunity, access and solidarity (European Commission 2009). Because of this and because there appears to be little understanding of the idea in Albania (it is not alone; many other countries use the jargon and the rhetoric, but cannot really describe its practice), the international review team felt that it should advance some thoughts about the key issues and the accompanying challenges.

First, youth organisations should be expected to, and supported in, reflecting on and investing in their possible task of doing 'youth work'. Some will elect to continue to "work with young people" in a variety of ways, but that is not necessarily doing youth work. Youth work is about civil society and associational life, and the international review team did not hear statements from NGOs that this was part of their central mission. They did talk about their desire for participation, for themselves and for young people, but they did not seem to be at all clear about what they wanted that participation to achieve, nor what their position was towards other youth NGOs, towards government, towards young people and towards Albanian society. They functioned largely in their own particular channel.

Second, it is not at all clear how youth organisational and young people's associational life is organised and funded. There is obviously a variety of funding streams from governments and private sponsors in Germany, Italy, Sweden, Spain, Austria and the Netherlands, and international donors such as USAID, the World Bank, and UNICEF. But funding sources, structures, processes and distribution were the focus of a great deal of criticism, and the alleged lack of transparency, possible corruption, and likely "distortion" of strategic youth policy objectives was a source of concern to the international review team.

Third, the international review team recognises the value and contribution of youth NGOs. Nevertheless, like youth NGOs elsewhere, most Albanian youth organisations derive from, and tend to serve, students. Educated young adults organise them and they tend to provide for younger people who attend school. There were some exceptions to this rule, such as the Roma community centre in Tirana and a community initiative in the countryside (though not so far from Tirana). These latter initiatives should be more strongly supported, and their tasks and activities mapped, in order to inspire comparable developments in other communities and with other disadvantaged groups of young people. If this is not a proactive element of a youth strategy and the support structures for making things happen, then there are serious risks of "empowering the powerful", or strengthening the capabilities of those who are already reasonably included. Policy that simply aims to promote individual competence through voluntary engagement may enhance social mobility but ultimately weakens local communities. A more structured "youth-in-community" policy is needed; otherwise the young people with "get up and go" (initiative, enterprise, enthusiasm, motivation) will, as soon as they get the chance, have got up and gone.

Fourth, the social divide discussed above also plays out as a geographical divide. There may be some compensations in the countryside for the lack of penetration of public youth policies, because more traditional structures of the family, school and local community may exercise a protective and supportive effect. The role of a priest, imam and teacher in resolving the blood feud case in Shkodra is a case in point. (Indeed, the "social" function of religion was something that impressed the international review team.) However, many pointed out that "Tirana is Tirana, and then there is Albania". The international review team interpreted this to mean that many youth policy initiatives do find their way into operation in Tirana but do not stretch far from the capital. This leaves any analysis requiring some attention to at least three groups of young people with different policy needs: the most privileged, in Tirana and able to access the provision available; those in the countryside, devoid of the same services, but still accessing support based on families, communities and culture; and those in Tirana who are excluded (or self-excluded) from youth policy provision. Sub-categories of this typology would no doubt apply to young people in each of the regions of Albania and their major towns. The question implied from all this is a simple one demanding a complex answer: to what extent does Albania want to level the playing field for its young people? Does it want to identify an essential "youth offer" (around, for example, education and training, health advice and information, leisure-time activity and engagement, opportunities for participation, access to information and care and protection) that should be extended to all young people in the country? Does it want to prioritise those groups of young people who may need these things most (after all, many young people get these things as a matter of course, or because they seek them out)? It seems to the international review team that the role of the planned National Youth Centre and its regional satellites could be critical to the shaping and delivery of such provision, once the principles governing that have been properly worked out.

In terms of the media, the international review team did not learn very much. We do know that many young people in Albania still have no, or limited access to the Internet.[33] And we also know that the media is eager to promote models of instant fame and material success that can produce pernicious role models for young people. Many people commented on this.

Returning to the National Youth Centre, the international review team suggests that, irrespective of detail, it should take on the following strategic responsibilities:

- the monitoring and validation of training for "youth workers";
- the provision of information to those working with young people;
- the provision of information for young people;
- the provision of support for the participation and engagement of young people;
- the co-ordination of relationships between the governmental and NGO sectors;
- the provision of advice on the distribution of grants;
- the development of international work.

---

33. The ministry wanted to note that "based on statistics more than 75% of young people in Albania have access to the Internet". Other sources would dispute this figure and, further, there are matters of more qualitative interpretation of the meaning of the concept and reality of "access".

These are but preliminary suggestions, but they would appear to capture some of the essential dimensions of youth policy and such strategic responsibility would help to enable and ensure the framework for a more coherent and structured approach to youth policy development and implementation in Albania.

## Looking to the future

"Our parents enjoyed some freedoms and were deprived of others. For example they had a wide circle of friends, more freedom to go out ... It was a stronger state, that had many laws and rules, and life was more secure. However, they were deprived of the freedom of speech, they could not express freely their opinion." (high-school boy, aged 17, Fier)

"If there were better living conditions I would stay here. ... It is not easy to be optimistic in this society." (compulsory-school girl, aged 13, Korca)

"But if we all leave, who will create the better future for Albania? We are the generation where hope rests for creating the future." (high-school boy, aged 17, Shkodra)

"Life has changed for better and worse. Years ago, students respected teachers, while today we do not. We do not fear the authority of the teacher any more and we talk back to the teachers." (schoolgirl, aged 12, Synej)

(Institute for Development of Research and Alternatives 2008, p. 204)

The vast majority of children think that Albania will be a better and much better place to live in the future. About half attribute this feeling to an improving economic situation. They want an Albania with a better economic situation, full employment, peace and no crime and delinquency (Institute for Development of Research and Alternatives 2008).

One of our respondents, who was deeply critical of the failure, for many reasons, of good visions to take root, encapsulated the views of many others with the following crisp summary of the prospects and achievements of Albanian youth policy:

The slogan that youth is the future is of course true, but we are not investing in them: education is not up to standard, there is the problem of youth unemployment. One thing we have lost is vocational training. In former times, we had very good vocational training. Nowadays it is easier to find experts in business management than a good plumber. There is a market for people with trades. Vocational training creates job opportunities quite quickly. If you have a supportive family, which many young people do have, with a good vocational education, you can set up a small business. With employment, one commendable effort of the government's last two terms has been the "brain-gain" initiative which, though not very effective, has been a good idea, trying to bring people back and make use of their experience, expertise and energy.

Conclusion

117

Another respondent from a youth project was rather more optimistic:

> I believe in the power of the young. I believe that in three years we will have achieved many things. Nothing is unachievable. If you look at the circumstances, it tends to give you a reason for pessimism. I look into the policy and then try to connect this with the realities. I try to find the space to create the best changes for the good of our country. We can see how young people come, and how they can become. I have noted the enhancement of their characters. We have seen many children who have not been through this youth centre and we know that our children are better prepared to be future leaders. One big issue is that post-communism we have built a huge generational gap, and now we have to establish inter-generational dialogue. Young people have to see Europe as closer and adopt a more European focused attitude and approach. One of the achievements now is that young people's attitudes are changing. Even parents, who now want to involve their children in the work that we do.

The AS@N, whom the international review team met for a second time towards the end of its second visit also expressed a sense of optimism, when asked how they thought things would be in some years' time. The following is a synthesis of the views of a number of those who commented:

> The focus of the government is now more on further education and training and on vocational education. We hope that this provision will improve and then we may see vocational education as being more attractive to young people than it is now. I think higher education, especially abroad, will still remain the dream for many young people. But we have come back and are now contributing to good outcomes for this society. This has involved quite a few challenges and difficult decisions for us. But in 10 years it will be a totally different picture. People will be able to travel more freely and they will not be trapped by the cost of the visa and the need to have made money to pay back the costs. And then, to use a saying we have in Albania, "It will be better to be the first in the village than the last in the city". If you limit people's desire, they think more about it. When they have a freer choice, I think people will go and see and then they will come back. People can see how things work elsewhere and then come back and do it here.

With regard to the implementation of the National Youth Strategy, many were extremely complimentary regarding its vision and content but few were convinced that it would lead to comprehensive action. Some of our respondents were asked what they would hope had materialised by around the year 2013 (the final year of the strategy). They mentioned:

- more focus on young people living abroad;
- the voices of young people to be heard in decision-making processes;
- fewer young people in the cafés and more young people in the libraries;
- the better promotion of education;
- more involvement in activities based on the protection of youth rights;
- the promotion by youth NGOs of young people voting and greater participation in political and civic life;

- more opportunities in education and employment;
- a dedicated proportion of the NGO budget being given over to youth NGOs (a fixed percentage);
- youth NGOs and politicians more daring and more open-minded in their initiatives.

Beyond the visions conveyed by somewhat older young people who were established activists in various NGOs, we asked a younger age group, members of a Youth Parliament, whether they felt that things were "looking good" for young people in Albania and what, if they had the chance, would they wish to tell their government. The follow is a synopsis of those views:

A lot still needs to be done. It has not been so enjoyable to be young so far. European Union integration will open possibilities for young people. The lifting of visa requirements has been a good step ...

The future looks bright, but not here in Albania; the politicians put flowers on things to make them look good, but schools and universities are still not very good, there are better opportunities abroad. Everything needs more effort that you can give.

I don't agree; we have great professors here in Albania.

I have a slightly different view: many students who have graduated here and then studied elsewhere have got good results, so the education here has been satisfactory.

If young people get involved in the sort of work we do, things will get better.

Even in your countries, you have your problems. We are realistic in what our challenges are. We are somehow in the middle!

Given the objectively still rather tough conditions facing so many young people, those we met were remarkably and admirably stoical and often moderately optimistic. They did not perceive specific obstacles in their way, but recognised that there could be, perhaps, insurmountable hurdles at some point: "we just don't know, we will see what life brings". Even the young Roma people we met in Shkodra were expressly more optimistic than their life circumstances suggested they should be: they were attending school (with the added incentive of food) and "looking forward to becoming someone in my life". Another individual in Durrës suggested that "things are going better now, even if it is a slow path, but we are cautiously optimistic". The young people we met did not seem to be obviously from particular or privileged backgrounds. They probably leaned towards that social category, but there were significant numbers whose mothers "stayed at home" and whose fathers were taxi drivers, car washers or farmers. What all these "active" young people shared was a determination to keep their options open and to be prepared for the challenges ahead. In that respect, they may have been rather different from the vast majority of young Albanians, if the perspectives of those working in youth policy, politics and NGOs are to be believed.

Conclusion

119

At all levels – national and regional government and amongst youth NGOs – there was talk of changing the mind-set of young people, "creating a new mentality" as one individual put it, especially by contact, exchange and experience beyond Albania's borders. For those who have had that opportunity, it has clearly worked, but equally clearly there is a majority of young people still locked, arguably trapped, within traditional assumptions and perspectives. The issue of reach, to a broader constituency of young people (especially more marginalised and disadvantaged groups) and beyond the boundaries of the bigger conurbations, remains a critical one.

Throughout each of its visits, the international review team recognised and respected the huge commitment of those in the youth field to their work. They were well-educated, generally used the same language, engaged in an impressively high level of debate, and projected a great deal of enthusiasm and activism. Whatever our criticisms and concerns – and we hope the issues will be considered and our mistakes forgiven – the international review team hopes that, with reasonably positive trends in social and economic development, this commitment and knowledge will be repaid through securing greater support from the government and more evidence of policy activation.

## Hope dies last

Youth policy in Albania ultimately has to find its path between contradictory traits that characterise some of the cultural traditions within the country: hospitality and revenge.

Commenting on these traditions, Vickers (2008, p. 255) writes:

> As always in Albania, settling accounts with the past plays a large part in the reality of the present causing the country to remain entrenched in the politics of conflict. There exists within the Albanian nation's cultural ethos a very simplistic message – *sa mbaj mua, une do te baj ty* – what you do to me, I will do to you. Hence the leadership of whichever political party holds office has attempted to discredit the previous regime. Such is the level of political tension, that both democrats and socialists remain deeply suspicious of each other's motives for entering any form of dialogue. The defining characteristics of social relations in Albania are still conflict and aggression.

Yet, paradoxically derived from the Kanun of the north – which successive regimes have sought to marginalise, if not eradicate, without success – there is a deeply ingrained code of behaviour regarding hospitality: *mikpritje*. Albanians, however poor, will offer you bread, salt and their heart: *buk e kryp e zemer* (De Waal 2007, p. 101). The vision of the National Youth Strategy is commendable, its application and implementation more questionable. The understanding and tolerance that flows from a culture of receptivity and hospitality remains undermined by an absence of public trust in the institutions of politics, law and justice, thus sustaining a culture of contestation and sometimes retribution. It is to be hoped, nonetheless, that the evident knowledge, expertise and commitment at youth policy level (within the ministries), coupled with the energy, enthusiasm and engagement of Albania's youth NGOs, will continue to build constructive and productive relationships for the ultimate benefit of Albania's young people and a next generation who will consolidate progress for the future and consign the chaos and corruption of the past to history.

As the international review team departed Albania, the newly reborn National Youth Council was finding its new direction. A parting remark is an apposite conclusion to this report:

> We need more of a balance and need to keep youth organisations at some distance from party politics. I want to increase the capacity of young people. We have a good strategy, we have some good laws, but we need the possibility for implementation. I want to invite people from other countries to speak with the Youth Council, "because hope dies last". We have to show that through democracy we can develop one country.

# Recommendations

### Recommendation 1
The international review team acknowledges the need for a greater educational focus on economic and enterprise education but believes the Albanian authorities should think about this not simply in terms of business innovation and entrepreneurship but as a pedagogical method for promoting initiative and creativity in young people. There can be education for, through and about enterprise.

### Recommendation 2
The international review team is concerned at the lack of understanding of the concept and methodologies of non-formal education which could be applied more, not only in the community but also in more formal educational structures, in order to address many of the "social" questions (of health, participation and democracy) that the Albanian authorities are currently addressing.

### Recommendation 3
The international review team sees many merits in the "brain-gain" programme, both to encourage the return of Albanian young people studying abroad and to establish career pathways for educated young people within the public administration. Such intellectual leadership may be required, but care should be taken to avoid strengthening what may be perceived as an already relatively privileged elite in whom disproportionate public resources are invested.

### Recommendation 4
Though impressed with the technical thinking of those in the health field, the international review team was concerned that health strategies are largely divorced from some of the wider social and economic realities of young people's lives, which require more incorporation and focus if effective health strategies are to be developed and implemented. There were glimpses of such thinking, such as at the SOS Kinderdörfer International Children's Village where medical support for families and their children is part of the package of intervention that helps children to remain with their families, or assists them in returning to them.

**Recommendation 5**

The international review team would have liked to have learned more about the capacity of street-based NGOs to refer clients to more mainstream, state-funded service provision.

**Recommendation 6**

Researching 'invisible' populations always, inevitably, presents methodological challenges, but a stronger evidence base on drug use, sexually transmitted infections, and the prevalence of HIV/Aids in Albania would seem to be urgently required.

**Recommendation 7**

Housing issues for young people are likely, in the relatively near future, to become a critical youth policy challenge. Dormitory provision will almost certainly not be enough, however important it may be today. Some creative thinking – perhaps around conversion of dilapidated buildings through vocational training initiatives, or even self-build schemes – is urgently needed.

**Recommendation 8**

The international review team was impressed with the work and innovation of SOS Kinderdörfer International, though it wondered how much of the "iceberg" of need its work really penetrated. Its significant message, nevertheless, is that with appropriate support, young people who are disconnected from their families can achieve in education, find suitable and secure employment, live in stable housing arrangements, and build productive relationships. This is an important lesson for the government, which should encourage it to consider extending the age range across which it supports young people who have formerly been in need of public care.

**Recommendation 9**

Given the very unique religious traditions in Albania, there is enormous potential for faith groups to make a contribution to the "social" sphere within which young people are growing up. The international review team had only glimpses of this potential – from remarks made by respondents, and from the role of faith leaders in the resolution of the blood feud dispute – but feels that more consideration should be given to it.

**Recommendation 10**

The international review team had serious concerns about the apparent absence of any regional economic development strategy in Albania. The out-migration of young people from more remote and rural communities is a common feature of many countries, but it is possible to think about "growth centre" strategies, in the interests of social, cultural and economic "rescue", if rural communities are not to suffer from demographic imbalance and ultimately die out.

**Recommendation 11**
The international review team felt that, despite the Albanian people's generally tolerant attitudes and particular history in relation to minorities, various minorities remain excluded from even the policy dialogue and others are subjected to considerable rhetoric but apparently limited intervention. Across a range of policy domains, more targeted and concerted efforts seem to be required.

**Recommendation 12**
The international review team recommends that greater efforts are made in legislation and education to develop a better understanding of and commitment to the idea of making a voluntary commitment to the "social" needs of others, especially more isolated, marginalised and disadvantaged young people.

**Recommendation 13**
The international review team commends the explicit formal position on gender equality and the areas where this is clearly also a reality. However, it believes that in some areas and sectors of activity, a more proactive strategy is required to challenge prevailing traditions, assumptions and stereotypes.

**Recommendation 14**
The international review team felt that more robust research is required to detect what kinds of proportions of those considered to require "social inclusion" are served by current state and NGO initiatives and the degree to which some "flagship" measures have the potential to be emulated with other groups, in other parts of the country, or on different issues.

**Recommendation 15**
The international review team is not persuaded that if something is enshrined in law in Albania, it happens. Law can be as obstructing as it can be enabling. There appears to be something of an obsession with legislative process: better and fewer laws might be a simple recommendation.

**Recommendation 16**
The international review team believes that an independent grant-giving structure for the youth NGO sector is urgently needed, to advise on the distribution of governmental resources and to act as a sounding board for other potential donors. There are models of this kind from other countries. In Albania, given the prevailing perspectives on recent history, it is likely to be the only way of restoring trust and confidence in funding mechanisms.

**Recommendation 17**
The international review team believes that, for the potential of youth policy delivery to be properly strengthened, there needs to be a stronger commitment to the funding of established youth NGOs, more robust regional and local youth strategies, a more confident governmental lead, better cross-sectoral co-operation at various levels and improved dissemination of ideas and good practice.

Recommendations

### Recommendation 18

The framework for youth participation that has been established in Albania is impressive. There appears to be real commitment to this issue and youth NGOs, with some serious support from international donors, have worked hard on implementation. There are weaknesses in most of the structures, however, which do require attention. Conceptually, the rationale was rarely articulated, beyond the UNCRC, though there are many other reasons for supporting youth participation. Operationally, there were issues about what young people actually did, what they said, who they said it to and what the results were. There are some exemplary stories, but the whole architecture of youth participation now needs cementing into a stronger infrastructure.

### Recommendation 19

General calls for "better information" suggest an absence of more calibrated understanding of the role of information in youth policy – both for youth professionals and for young people. The international review team believes that more structured and focused information systems are required for both constituencies but, before these are developed, more clarity of thought is required about their objectives, audiences and methodologies.

### Recommendation 20

New technologies do offer alternative possibilities for young people to communicate and network. However, there remains a strong case for some dedicated physical space at the local level where young people can gather – associate – and engage in or plan activities as well as simply "hang around", talk and enjoy themselves. Such space is ideally sheltered – and therefore buildings are desirable – but alternatives such as sports fields (or the corners of them!) or outdoor seating areas with an optional bad weather cover, rather like the ubiquitous car washing spaces, would be another possibility.

### Recommendation 21

The international review team strongly recommends the further development of community-based provision for young offenders – for both supervision and surveillance – as an alternative to custody, a platform for restorative justice and as a mechanism for rehabilitation and re-integration.

# Bibliography

Albania National Youth Strategy (2009), PowerPoint presentation.

Albanian Association of Psychologists (2008), *National Assessment of the Drug and Substance Abuse Problem in Albania: Situation, Trends, Reasons,* supported by UNICEF.

Albanian Helsinki Committee (no date), *Njihni te drejtat tuaja* (human rights booklet for imprisoned offenders – in Albanian).

Association for Women and Children (2002), *Raising the Awareness of the Public Opinion on the Women's Role as Partner in the Economical, Political and Social Life of the Community,* Tirana: Association for Women and Children.

Banton M. (1972), *Racial Minorities,* Fontana, London.

BBC (2009), *Country Profile: Albania.*

Belton B. (2010), *Radical Youth Work: Developing critical perspectives and professional judgement,* Russell House Publishing, Lyme Regis.

Billings A. (2008), *God and Community Cohesion: Help or hindrance?* SPCK, London.

Breen P., Shiønnemann M-E., Nurse L., Azzopardi A., Lagree J-C. and Lauritzen P. (2003), *Youth Policy in Lithuania: Report by an international panel of experts appointed by the Council of Europe,* Council of Europe Publishing, Strasbourg.

*Budapest Times,* 5-11 October 2009, 'Another reason to stay healthy'.

Bushat Commune (2008), *Local Environment Action Plan,* Gent Grafik, Tirana.

Coussée F. (2008), *A Century of Youth Work Policy,* Academia Press, Gent.

Department of Education and Science (1982), *Experience and Participation: Report of the Review Group on the Youth Service in England,* HMSO, London.

De Waal C. (2007), *Albania Today: A portrait of post-communist turbulence,* I.B. Tauris, London.

European Commission (2002), *A New Impetus for European Youth – White Paper,* European Commission, Brussels.

European Commission (2009), *An EU Strategy for Youth: Investing and empowering – A renewed open method of coordination to address youth challenges and opportunities,* European Commission, Brussels.

European Youth Forum (2007), *Youth Work Development Report on the Study Visit to Albania, 20-23 May 2007,* Youth Forum Jeunesse, Brussels.

Facts about Albania (2009), at www.marts100.com/alb_fact.htm.

Foreign and Commonwealth Office (2009), *Albania.*

Gjeka B. (2009), *Volunteerism Perceptions and Realities in the Albanian Youth Sector,* UN Volunteers/UNDP, Tirana.

*The Guardian,* 23 November 2009, 'Welcome to the 28th state'.

Institute for Development of Research and Alternatives (2008), *Albania Young Voices: National study,* UNICEF, Tirana.

Institute of Public Health (2009), *Project Proposal.*

Jamieson I., Hunt D., Richards B. and Williamson H. (1988), *The Mini-Enterprise in Schools Project: An evaluation,* Department of Trade and Industry, London.

Jasiukaityté V. and Reiter H. (2002), *Youth Policy in Transformation: Lithuanian youth policy review,* State Council for Youth Affairs, Vilnius.

KRSH (2009) Press Release: *Civil Society reaffirms the will for re-establishing the Albanian Youth Council.*

Milmeister M. and Williamson H. (eds) (2006), *Dialogues and Networks: Organising exchanges between youth field actors,* Editions Phi, Luxembourg.

Ministry of Labour, Social Affairs and Equal Opportunities (2007), *Sectoral Strategy on Employment and Vocational Training 2007-2013.*

Ministry of Tourism, Culture, Youth and Sports (2006), *National Youth Strategy 2007-2013.*

Nientied P. (1998), "The question of town and regional planning in Albania", *Habitat International,* Vol. 22, No. 1, pp. 41-47.

OSCE (2009), *Probation Project in Albania Evaluation Report: Assessment of the current stage of introducing probation in Albania,* OSCE, Tirana.

Orgocka A. and Jovanovic J. (2006), "Identity exploration and commitment of Albanian youth as a function of social opportunity structure", *European Psychologist*, Vol. 11, No. 4, pp. 268-76.

Partners–Albania (Center for Change and Conflict Management) (2005), *Advocacy Capacities of the Albanian NPO Sector: Assessment report*, Partners Albania, Tirana.

Partners–Albania (Center for Change and Conflict Management) (c.2006), *Youth lidership* [sic].

Partners–Albania (Center for Change and Conflict Management) (2008), *Sustainability, Partnership, Knowledge, Skills* (training booklet).

Rees G. and Rees T. (1992), "Educating for the 'enterprise economy': a critical review", in P. Brown and H. Lauder (eds), *Education for Economic Survival*, Routledge, London.

Rutter M. and Smith D. (eds) (1994), *Psycho-Social Disorders in Young People: Time trends and their causes*, Heinemann, London.

*Shkodra: The region of privacy* (free tourist guide).

www.sos-childrensvillages.org/Where-we-help/Europe/Albania.

SOS Kinderdörfer International (no date), *Preparation for Independent Living*.

UNFPA (2008), *Mission Report*.

U.S. Central Intelligence Agency, *World Factbook* (2009), 'Albania'.

U.S. Department of State (2008), *Background Note: Albania*, Bureau of European and Eurasian Affairs.

Verschelden G., Coussée F., Van de Walle T. and Williamson H. (eds) (2009), *The History of Youth Work in Europe: Relevance for today's youth work policy*, Council of Europe Publishing, Strasbourg.

Vickers M. (1999), *The Albanians: A modern history*, I.B. Tauris, London.

Wikipedia (2009), *Albania*.

Williamson H. (2002), *Supporting Young People in Europe: Principles, policy and practice*, Council of Europe Publishing, Strasbourg.

Williamson H. (2008), *Supporting Young People in Europe, Vol. 2*, Council of Europe Publishing, Strasbourg.

Williamson H., Hoskins B. and Boetzelen P. (eds) (2005), *Charting the Landscape of European Youth Voluntary Activities*, Council of Europe Publishing, Strasbourg.

*World Factbook* (2009), Albania.

Youth Parliament of Tirana (2009), *What is Done and What is Planned to be Done*.

Bibliography

# Appendix 1 - Programme of the first visit to Albania

| | | |
|---|---|---|
| **Tuesday 22 September** | 09:00-11:15 | Ministry of Tourism, Culture, Youth and Sports; discussions with the Youth Policies Department. |
| | 11:30-13:00 | Ministry of Education: Mr Fatmir Vejsiu, Director of Secondary Education Department. |
| | 14:30-18:00 | Youth Council, national youth organisations: Students' Government, National Students Council, Youth Parliament. |
| **Wednesday 23 September** | 09:30-10:30 | Ministry of Employment, Social Affairs and Equal Opportunities: Ms Genta Qosja, Mr Stavri Lako, Directorate of Employment Policies. |
| | 11:00-13:00 | Ministry of Health: Mr Arjan Harxhi, Director General of Health Planning Policies Department, Mr Gazmend Bejtja, Director of the Public Health Department. |
| | 14:30-15:30 | Soros Foundation. |
| | 16:00-18:00 | Visit to a youth project (MOKO – Museum of the Objects of Communism). |
| **Thursday 24 September** | 09:30-11:00 | Ministry of Justice: Mr Miran Kopani. |
| | 11:30-13:00 | Ministry of Employment, Social Affairs and Equal Opportunities, Department of Migration. |
| | 14:30-16:30 | International NGOs: Save the Children, UNICEF. |
| | 17:00-18:00 | National NGOs: Albanian branch of European Youth Parliament, AS@N, Start and Go, SIFE, KRIIK Albania, Beyond the Barriers, Action+. |

| Friday 25 September | 09:30-11:00 | Ministry of Integration: Ms Patris Hida-Kraja, Director, Department of Institutional Support to the Integration Process. |
|---|---|---|
| | 11:30-13:00 | Ms Juliana Hoxha, Partners Albania. |
| | 14:30-16:30 | Youth practitioners: Ms Alma Cullhaj, Ms Ana Dervishi, representing Action+. |
| | 16:30-18:00 | Team work. |
| Saturday 26 September | 11:00-11:30 | Meeting with Minister Ferdinand Xhaferaj. |

# Appendix 2 - Programme of the second visit to Albania

| | | |
|---|---|---|
| **Tuesday 24 November** | 09:30-10:00 | Meeting with Ms Migena Reçi, Director of Youth Policies Department. |
| | 10:15-11:30 | Meeting with Mrs Lajla Pernaska, Parliament Committee for Health and Youth. |
| | 11:45-13:00 | Meeting with professional trainers. |
| | 14:45-18:00 | Split visit in two groups:<br>– youth crime: prison staff and inmates in Kavaja.<br>– SOS Kinderdörfer, Tirana, and Sports Association, Tirana. |
| **Wednesday 25 November** | 09:30-10:30 | Vocational education school "Beqir Cela", Shkozet Durrës. |
| | 11:00-12:00 | Youth Parliament Durrës. |
| | 15:00-17:00 | Youth Centre Fier: Pilot project "Youth Agent for Change". |
| **Thursday 26 November** | 10:30-11:00 | Meeting with Mr Lorenc Luka, Mayor of Shkodra. |
| | 11:30-13:00 | Meeting with Mr Zef Hila, Head of Commune of Bushat, Citizens and Youth. |
| | 13:00-14:00 | Visit to a blood feud family in Bushat. |
| | 16:00-17:30 | Visit to community project by local NGOs in Shkodra (Roma and Egyptians). |
| **Friday 27 November** | 09:00-10:30 | Visit to Roma community in Tirana. |
| | 11:00-12:30 | Community social centre for children with limited abilities, Tirana-Kombinat. |
| | 16:00-17:00 | Review meeting with the ministry. |
| | 17:00-18:00 | Meeting with Albanian Youth Council representatives. |

# Sales agents for publications of the Council of Europe
# Agents de vente des publications du Conseil de l'Europe

**BELGIUM/BELGIQUE**
La Librairie Européenne -
The European Bookshop
Rue de l'Orme, 1
BE-1040 BRUXELLES
Tel.: +32 (0)2 231 04 35
Fax: +32 (0)2 735 08 60
E-mail: order@libeurop.be
http://www.libeurop.be

Jean De Lannoy/DL Services
Avenue du Roi 202 Koningslaan
BE-1190 BRUXELLES
Tel.: +32 (0)2 538 43 08
Fax: +32 (0)2 538 08 41
E-mail: jean.de.lannoy@dl-servi.com
http://www.jean-de-lannoy.be

**BOSNIA AND HERZEGOVINA/
BOSNIE-HERZÉGOVINE**
Robert's Plus d.o.o.
Marka Maruliça 2/V
BA-71000, SARAJEVO
Tel.: + 387 33 640 818
Fax: + 387 33 640 818
E-mail: robertsplus@bih.net.ba

**CANADA**
Renouf Publishing Co. Ltd.
1-5369 Canotek Road
CA-OTTAWA, Ontario K1J 9J3
Tel.: +1 613 745 2665
Fax: +1 613 745 7660
Toll-Free Tel.: (866) 767-6766
E-mail: order.dept@renoufbooks.com
http://www.renoufbooks.com

**CROATIA/CROATIE**
Robert's Plus d.o.o.
Marasoviçeva 67
HR-21000, SPLIT
Tel.: + 385 21 315 800, 801, 802, 803
Fax: + 385 21 315 804
E-mail: robertsplus@robertsplus.hr

**CZECH REPUBLIC/
RÉPUBLIQUE TCHÈQUE**
Suweco CZ, s.r.o.
Klecakova 347
CZ-180 21 PRAHA 9
Tel.: +420 2 424 59 204
Fax: +420 2 848 21 646
E-mail: import@suweco.cz
http://www.suweco.cz

**DENMARK/DANEMARK**
GAD
Vimmelskaftet 32
DK-1161 KØBENHAVN K
Tel.: +45 77 66 60 00
Fax: +45 77 66 60 01
E-mail: gad@gad.dk
http://www.gad.dk

**FINLAND/FINLANDE**
Akateeminen Kirjakauppa
PO Box 128
Keskuskatu 1
FI-00100 HELSINKI
Tel.: +358 (0)9 121 4430
Fax: +358 (0)9 121 4242
E-mail: akatilaus@akateeminen.com
http://www.akateeminen.com

**FRANCE**
La Documentation française
(diffusion/distribution France entière)
124, rue Henri Barbusse
FR-93308 AUBERVILLIERS CEDEX
Tél.: +33 (0)1 40 15 70 00
Fax: +33 (0)1 40 15 68 00
E-mail: commande@ladocumentationfrancaise.fr
http://www.ladocumentationfrancaise.fr

Librairie Kléber
1 rue des Francs Bourgeois
FR-67000 STRASBOURG
Tel.: +33 (0)3 88 15 78 88
Fax: +33 (0)3 88 15 78 80
E-mail: librairie-kleber@coe.int
http://www.librairie-kleber.com

**GERMANY/ALLEMAGNE
AUSTRIA/AUTRICHE**
UNO Verlag GmbH
August-Bebel-Allee 6
DE-53175 BONN
Tel.: +49 (0)228 94 90 20
Fax: +49 (0)228 94 90 222
E-mail: bestellung@uno-verlag.de
http://www.uno-verlag.de

**GREECE/GRÈCE**
Librairie Kauffmann s.a.
Stadiou 28
GR-105 64 ATHINAI
Tel.: +30 210 32 55 321
Fax.: +30 210 32 30 320
E-mail: ord@otenet.gr
http://www.kauffmann.gr

**HUNGARY/HONGRIE**
Euro Info Service
Pannónia u. 58.
PF. 1039
HU-1136 BUDAPEST
Tel.: +36 1 329 2170
Fax: +36 1 349 2053
E-mail: euroinfo@euroinfo.hu
http://www.euroinfo.hu

**ITALY/ITALIE**
Licosa SpA
Via Duca di Calabria, 1/1
IT-50125 FIRENZE
Tel.: +39 0556 483215
Fax: +39 0556 41257
E-mail: licosa@licosa.com
http://www.licosa.com

**MEXICO/MEXIQUE**
Mundi-Prensa México, S.A. De C.V.
Río Pánuco, 141 Delegacíon Cuauhtémoc
MX-06500 MÉXICO, D.F.
Tel.: +52 (01)55 55 33 56 58
Fax: +52 (01)55 55 14 67 99
E-mail: mundiprensa@mundiprensa.com.mx
http://www.mundiprensa.com.mx

**NETHERLANDS/PAYS-BAS**
Roodveldt Import BV
Nieuwe Hemweg 50
NE-1013 CX AMSTERDAM
Tel.: + 31 20 622 8035
Fax.: + 31 20 625 5493
Website: www.publidis.org
Email: orders@publidis.org

**NORWAY/NORVÈGE**
Akademika
Postboks 84 Blindern
NO-0314 OSLO
Tel.: +47 2 218 8100
Fax: +47 2 218 8103
E-mail: support@akademika.no
http://www.akademika.no

**POLAND/POLOGNE**
Ars Polona JSC
25 Obroncow Street
PL-03-933 WARSZAWA
Tel.: +48 (0)22 509 86 00
Fax: +48 (0)22 509 86 10
E-mail: arspolona@arspolona.com.pl
http://www.arspolona.com.pl

**PORTUGAL**
Livraria Portugal
(Dias & Andrade, Lda.)
Rua do Carmo, 70
PT-1200-094 LISBOA
Tel.: +351 21 347 42 82 / 85
Fax: +351 21 347 02 64
E-mail: info@livrariaportugal.pt
http://www.livrariaportugal.pt

**RUSSIAN FEDERATION/
FÉDÉRATION DE RUSSIE**
Ves Mir
17b, Butlerova ul.
RU-101000 MOSCOW
Tel.: +7 495 739 0971
Fax: +7 495 739 0971
E-mail: orders@vesmirbooks.ru
http://www.vesmirbooks.ru

**SPAIN/ESPAGNE**
Mundi-Prensa Libros, s.a.
Castelló, 37
ES-28001 MADRID
Tel.: +34 914 36 37 00
Fax: +34 915 75 39 98
E-mail: libreria@mundiprensa.es
http://www.mundiprensa.com

**SWITZERLAND/SUISSE**
Planetis Sàrl
16 chemin des Pins
CH-1273 ARZIER
Tel.: +41 22 366 51 77
Fax: +41 22 366 51 78
E-mail: info@planetis.ch

**UNITED KINGDOM/ROYAUME-UNI**
The Stationery Office Ltd
PO Box 29
GB-NORWICH NR3 1GN
Tel.: +44 (0)870 600 5522
Fax: +44 (0)870 600 5533
E-mail: book.enquiries@tso.co.uk
http://www.tsoshop.co.uk

**UNITED STATES and CANADA/
ÉTATS-UNIS et CANADA**
Manhattan Publishing Co
2036 Albany Post Road
USA-10520 CROTON ON HUDSON, NY
Tel.: +1 914 271 5194
Fax: +1 914 271 5886
E-mail: coe@manhattanpublishing.coe
http://www.manhattanpublishing.com

## Council of Europe Publishing/Editions du Conseil de l'Europe
FR-67075 STRASBOURG Cedex
Tel.: +33 (0)3 88 41 25 81 – Fax: +33 (0)3 88 41 39 10 – E-mail: publishing@coe.int – Website: http://book.coe.int